ETHNICITY AND ORGANIZATIONAL DIVERSITY

*A Study of Social Cognition
and Psychological Climate Perception*

Wendy V. Lewis Chung

University Press of America, Inc.
Lanham • New York • London

Copyright © 1997 by
University Press of America,® Inc.
4720 Boston Way
Lanham, Maryland 20706

3 Henrietta Street
London, WC2E 8LU England

Library of Congress Cataloging-in-Publication Data

Chung, Wendy V. Lewis.
Ethnicity and organizational diversity : a study of social cognition and
psychological climate perception / Wendy V. Lewis Chung.
p.   cm.
Includes bibliographical references and index.
1. Social perception. 2. College students--Psychology. 3.
Ethnopsychology. I. Title.
BF323.S63C48 1996   155.8'2--dc20   96-41350 CIP

ISBN 0-7618-0528-1 (cloth: alk. ppr.)

This book is dedicated to:

my husband, Owen
my son, Christopher and
my mother, Maria Alexander

TABLE OF CONTENTS

LIST OF FIGURES

LIST OF TABLES

Preface

Organizations' leaders are investing inordinate amounts of time and money on preparing their organizations for diversity. However, a significant portion of these diversity efforts are devoted to information-based training sessions and the inclusion of diversity issues into college curricula. Diversity trainers ignore the fact that, as Thomas aptly puts it, "You can't grow peaches on an oak tree. To grow peaches the roots must be peach friendly" (p. A-14). In order to train employees to accept and respect diversity, these efforts must occur within an organization whose culture is diversity-friendly. Despite this, most diversity training and curriculum inclusion efforts occur within organizations whose cultures endorse monoculturalism. Diversity specialists ignore the salience of not only the organization's culture in the success of true organizational diversity but also the employees' perception of situations and events in the organization's environment.

This text evolves from intensive and extensive investigation of the relationship between ethnicity and the development of psychological climate perception. Experimental research is conducted among and within three different ethnic groups of students in a university environment to determine if there is interethnicity and intraethnicity variance in perception of diversity issues within that environment. The core postulation of this research is that the keys to ultimate organizational diversity exist in the treatment of the organization's culture and, most importantly, in the careful attention to employees' perception of issues of diversity in the organization's climate.

Because of its statistically significant results, the research helps us to understand how the ethnicity of organizational members influences the development of their psychological climate (pc) perception. PC perception refers to the individual's cognitive representation of proximal environments, expressed in terms that represent the personal and acquired meaning of environments to individuals (James & Sells, 1981); in other words, individuals assign psychological meaning to environmental attributes and events. This study further posits that psychological climate perception is a function of the individual's ethnicity which is defined by Longstreet (1978) as the outcome of a person's national, scholastic, and family ethnicities.

In the quest to determine the role that ethnicity plays in the development of an individual's psychological climate (PC) perception, this research proceeds from a strong conceptual framework which the author develops based on an equally strong theoretical foundation. The framework suggests that psychological climate (pc) perceptions are a function of the individual's interaction with his/her national, scholastic, and family ethnicities (Longstreet, 1978) which provides a cognitive structure that shapes his/her perception of the world. It further claims that as individuals interact with their environment, they employ cognitive constructions as they give psychological meaning to the situations and events encountered in the environment in which they function (James & Jones, 1974).

Part 1 of this book analyzes the two dominant theories -ethnicity and perception- advanced in the conceptual framework of this study and presents an extensive review of relevant theories. Chapter 1 introduces the research by detailing the background of the research problem. Chapter 2 advances the conceptual and philosophical framework employed in this study and provides operational definitions of the ethnicity and perception theories. Chapter 3 extensively reviews literature critical to the theoretical foundation that underlies the relationship between ethnicity and psychological climate perceptions. It also examines the philosophical congruence between symbolic interactionism and psychological climate perception theories. Chapter 4 examines the cognitive and ethnic development of African Americans, Euro-Americans, and Latin Americans in the United States. It analyzes the historical background of these groups and examines their family, national, and scholastic evolution.

In order to apply the theoretical concepts that were examined and detailed in part 1 of this text, part 2 details an experimental study that investigates the relationship between ethnicity and the development of psychological climate perceptions among three ethnic groups of students on a college campus. Chapter 5 details the procedures employed in this investigation. It specifically describes the sample selection and instrumentation procedures and presents the study's results. Chapter 6 discusses the implications of the study's results for the study's research questions, while chapter 7 discusses the implications of the results for the quest for organizational diversity, the theoretical implications of the results, the limitations of the study, and it recommends areas for further research.

Acknowledgments

There is a wonderful combination of ideas, people, and experiences that has served to make the realization of this book possible. There is no way to adequately thank all those to whom I feel indebted; however, there are those who deserve special mention for their love, inspiration, and support.

First, I especially thank my mother, Maria B. Alexander, whose support inspired me as it has through my many years of study and research and whose love continues to inspire me throughout my life. Special thanks to my dear husband and friend, Owen A. Chung, whose technical assistance, unfailing support and patience helped me through the completion of this document and my deepest thanks to my son, Christopher B. Chung, whose love motivated me through this project.

I offer special thanks to Carol Dix and Linda Feeney for their invaluable computer assistance in the completion of the study. I also want to express my appreciation to Ritchard M'Bayo whose editorial expertise and technical assistance contributed to the completion of this volume.

I particularly express my gratitude to two academic and professional advisers, Dr. Leroy Wells and Dr. Marcia Clinckscales, for their expertise and guidance in the completion of this manuscript.

Finally, I owe a special debt of thanks to the students who took time off from their very busy schedules during the semester's end to participate in this study.

PART ONE

CHAPTER 1

Organizational Demands Created by Changing National Demographics: An Introduction

Nineteen eighty-eight marked the beginning of the emergence of America's "one-third of a nation" — the blacks, Hispanics, American Indians, and Asian-Americans who constitute the minority population. The visibility of these groups in the "American tapestry" is growing rapidly. The American Council of Education (1988) projects that by the year 2000, one-third of all school-age children will fall into this category. Between 1985 and 2000, minority workers will make up one-third of the net additions to the United States (US) labor force and by the turn of the century, 21.8 million of the 140.4 million people in the labor force will be nonwhite.

These statistics reflect not only the increasing cultural diversity of the nation but also a shift in demographics. They also suggest a consequent need for a nation to instrument changes to facilitate this growing trend of cultural diversity. Already, major corporations have embarked on programs of change as they attempt to realign their corporate cultures to support cultural diversity. One such company is Allstate Insurance whose Assistant Vice-President of human resources is quoted by Glasheen (1989) as saying:

> We don't want affirmative action any more; we want true cultural diversity. In the past most companies have hired minorities and women with the goal of processing them to fit in with the existing corporate cultures. That often results in frustration. Our aim is to create a culture where you value the differences; where you take these heterogeneous elements and have them be the culture — where nobody is either advantaged or disadvantaged by their ethnic background. (p.30)

In essence, proactive planning in all industries must be rooted in the fact that in the twenty-first century, according to Henry (1990), "racial and ethnic groups in the US will outnumber whites for the first time" (p.28). The "browning of America" will impact all aspects of society, including politics, education, religion, industry, and most importantly, values and culture. The American culture will experience an inevitable shift.

Henry quotes from Molefi Asante, Chairman of the Department of African-American studies at Temple University who states: "Once America was a microcosm of European nationalities, today America is a microcosm of the world" (p.29). Currently, one out of four Americans defines himself/herself as Hispanic or nonwhite. With a persistence of current immigration trends and birth rates, residents who are Hispanic or nonwhite will by 2020 have more than doubled to almost 115 million (See Table 1:1), while the white population numbers will stagnate. Henry states that by the end of the twentieth century, the Hispanic population will have increased by 21%, Asian by 22%, blacks by almost 12% and whites by just over 2% (p.29).

The relationship between subcultural strength and size ought to be of critical concern to market planners or organizations involved in proactive planning; in other words, they should be concerned about whether the strength of these subcultures will decrease as the sizes increase. However, current trends indicate the reverse. In the past, generations of immigrants felt the need to become proficient in English in order to survive in the US. Many Hispanics now maintain that Spanish is inseparable from their cultural values and identity so they remain bilingual or primarily Spanish-speaking. One striking example is that of the His-

YEAR	White non-Hispanic %	Black %	Hispanic %	Asian and Other %
1950	86.2	9.9	2.7	1.2
1987	77.6	12.1	7.9	2.4
2020	69.5	14.3	11.1	5.0

Table 1.1: U.S. Racial and Ethnic Composition, 1950-2020
Source: U.S. Bureau of Census

panic populations in Miami, Florida, that are primarily Spanish-speaking. Certainly, there is that need to preserve the strength of their subcultural identities as they deem any legislation to make English the only official language a response to the increase in and growing influence of Hispanics (Henry III, 1990, p.29). Femminella (1979) observes that first-, second-, and third-generation Hispanics, unlike other ethnic groups, seem to maintain their ethnic identity throughout the years. Hispanic migration to the US is continuous and increasing. As larger numbers of Hispanics arrive, they bring with them ethnic values, beliefs, and practices which seem to reinforce the already established Hispanic culture in the US. The strength of the culture protects the members against assimilation. This fact has implications for the American "melting pot" philosophy. With continually growing ethnic groups that are increasing not only in size but strength major institutions and corporations will have to re-adjust their missions.

A New Identity?

Certainly, this issue of a new national culture has been met with diverse and opposing opinions among scholars. Responses to the phenomenon can be categorized into traditionalist and nontraditionalist views. The traditionalists argue that it is critical for a society to have one universally accepted set of values. They propose that new arrivals must be pressured to conform or assimilate to the existing culture. Henry quotes Allan Bloom, traditionalist and author, as saying, "Obviously, the future of America can't be sustained if people keep their own ways and remain perpetual outsiders. The society has got to turn them into Americans. There are natural fears that today's immigrants may be too much of a cultural stretch for a nation based on Western values" (p. 31). Julian Simons, professor at the University of Maryland, yet another traditionalist quoted by Henry, suggests that "the life and institutions here shape immigrants and not vice versa. This business about immigrants changing our institutions and our basic ways of life is 'hogwash.' It's nativist scare talk" (p.31). Also, historian Thomas Bender, when interviewed by Henry challenges this argument as he posits that "it should be the ever changing outcome of a continuing contest among social groups and ideas for the power to define public culture." He suggests that if the center no longer holds, it must be redefined (p.31).

The reality of the "browning of America" and its profound impact must be realized. The projected shift in not only the cultural but the racial mix of the US in the 2000s demands that politicians, economists, legislators, educators, and other public servants prepare to readjust missions and policies to facilitate this new American mix, which will inevitably pervade all sectors of the society. The number of members in the minority groups will increase, resulting in their increase as consumers, voters, taxpayers, employees and students and consequently, sparking growth in other demographic areas.

The increase in and the quality of interactions among culturally diverse groups can no longer be ignored. Measures must be taken to promote cultural understanding and sensitivity among the diverse groups. Already mentioned is the fact that a few major corporations such as Apple Computer and Allstate Insurance have taken the initiative to realign corporate cultures to meet this growing demand. This is truly a step in the right direction; however, a more fundamental change is necessary. Diversity must become an inherent part of organizations' culture thus creating organizational climates that facilitate successful diversity efforts. The success of this type of climate is a function of the attitudes and perceptions of organizational members who ought to truly value and respect diversity. This may require members to experience some cognitive and psychological changes in attitudes and perceptions toward ethnic differences. Since human resistance to change increases with human experience and age, the source that holds the potential for this type of change therefore lies in the educational institutions.

The impact of this demographic trend on education must not be ignored. The cultural mix of the nation will inevitably be echoed in the classrooms at all levels. The highly visible presence of cultural diversity will demand a need for educators to understand the psychological and cognitive processes that characterize the perceptions of ethnically different students in the educational institution. This need will be based on the reality that today, as Katz (1989) notes, "racism and other forms of oppression are woven into the cultural fabric of the United States.... Our racism has changed in form but not in function" (p. 2). Some ethnic groups continue to harbor varying degrees of resentment for cultural differences. With an understanding of the psychological and perceptual processes that students employ to give meaning to diversity issues, educators will be equipped to cultivate college/university climates that facilitate the understanding and valuing of cultural differences among all students.

The creation of diversity climates to support diversity efforts in education is important for two reasons: (1) Major corporations are readjusting their cultures to support the increasing cultural diversity of their clientele. In order to staff these corporations adequately and efficiently, educators must realign their education missions, values, and operating systems so that their graduates are adequately sensitized to meet the corporate demands for facilitating and understanding cultural diversity. Second, the enrollment increase in students across these minority groups will result in a climate in which sensitivities to cultural differences and values will become critical. This readjustment in educational missions will not only ensure culturally sensitized graduates but will also create a learning environment in which tensions caused by cultural differences are minimal.

The Potentialities of College Education in Pro-action

College environments offer fertile ground for the cultivation of a generation that can competently facilitate the current and future trends of increased cultural diversity. It is the educational institution that fertilizes the seeds of the corporate world, a world in which " the imagery of a 'global village' fosters a somewhat less ethnocentric posture ... one that promotes introspection" according to Smircich &Calas (1989, p. 230). A microcosm of that renowned "global village" is beginning to take shape in the US as current and continuing changes in the cultural diversity in demographics occur. According to Lynch (1988), "A culturally diverse society embraces a multiplicity of differing socialization and enculturation processes in the primary agencies of family and immediate community, which may be generative of predispositions to think, believe and act in ways that are sharply divergent from those of other groups" (p. 62). These divergent values and norms can consequently be inimical to those of the corporations that are proactively embarking on major corporate culture shifts. It is therefore the duty of the policy makers and mission builders of the educational institutions to align their objectives to meet the needs of corporations. They must provide them with graduates who are academically, intellectually, and socially sensitized to the permanence of multiculturalism and who are prepared to fit into the new corporate cultures that are aimed at satisfying the cultural divergence of the country.

Changes in college climates: a potential

With a commitment to realignment, educators must initially investigate if there are differences in existing psychological climate (PC) perceptions held by culturally different college/university students about their educational environment. If so, it should be determined how much of this perceptual difference can be attributed to ethnic heritage. Psychological climate measures the individual as the unit of analysis. It allows for the determination of those aspects of a college environment that are psychologically meaningful for the college student. This type of investigation allows for a broad range of assessments of the differing perceptions students hold about diversity issues in college life, the cognitive/psychological processes that are used to formulate these perceptions, and the implications these perceptions may have for students' assessment or expectations of corporate life. In essence, it will provide information that will answer a variety of questions concerning culturally inspired differences in climate perception of the diverse cultural groups of students that comprise these institutions.

Feldman (1971) writes that much effort has been expended in the measurement of university climate. More specifically, research in this area reflects a wide array of investigations conducted in the perceptions of university climate in different subgroups (black and white) within the university (Pfeifer & Schneider, 1974; Pfeifer, 1976; Hedegard & Brown, 1969; Willie & Levy, 1972). These investigations concluded that people in different groups (black and white) at the same university may function under different conditions and perceive climate differently. Pfeifer (1976) found a correlation between scholastic aptitude, perception of university climate, and college success for black and white students. However, a review of literature in the area has revealed an absence of research that investigates (1) psychological climate as it relates to the actual cause(s) of the differences in the climate perceptions among cultural groups and (2) the implications of these perceptions of college climate for their preparedness for diversity in the corporate world.

Understandably, past research efforts have excluded investigation into ethnic psychological factors that determine differences in perception of climate among college/university students and its implication for their preparedness for the evolving multiethnic corporate culture. This thrust toward corporate cultural shifts to fit a multiculturally diverse population is a relatively new one, and the consequent need to readjust school curricula to include multicultural education has been met with resistance. In the past half-century, however, much has been written on the different subcultural groups as they live in the US, are educated in US schools, communicate with each other, and cope with problems that result from the intercultural encounter between groups. Educational research lacks investigations that address the differences in the cognitive construction processes that affect psychological climate (PC) perception of ethnically different college-age students.

In essence, there is an absence of psychological climate (PC) research in the field of educational research. The study of psychological climate

(PC) provides investigation of this nature the opportunity to determine the student's cognitive representation of proximal environments, which is expressed in terms that represent the personal or acquired meaning to that student (James & Sells, 1981).

Psychological climate (PC): Gaps in research

Psychological climate and its correlates have been examined across organizational environments in an attempt to study behavior in organizations. This theory was developed primarily to study individuals' perception of work environments (James & Jones, 1974, 1976) although the assumptions underlying psychological climate theory were derived from many areas of psychology and the assumptions themselves are not limited to the work environment.

Psychological climate refers to the individual's cognitive representation of proximal environments, expressed in terms that represent the personal or acquired meaning of environments to individuals (James & Sells, 1981). It provides a step toward the formation of specific theoretical statements. These theories address the nature of the psychological processes that occur between the organizational situation and the attitudes and behavior of individual members of the organization. Psychological climate (PC) theory postulates that individuals tend to interpret situations in psychological terms. In other words, they assign psychological meaning to environmental attributes and events (Ekehammar, 1974; James et al. 1978; Schneider,1975).

Significant time has been invested in the development of theories, models, measurements techniques, and the determining of variables to describe the phenomenon. During the 1970s, a number of scholars such as Hornick, James and Jones (1977); James and Jones (1974,1976); James et al. (1979); James et al. (1978); Jones and James (1979); Jones, James and Bruni (1975) developed a research program to investigate bases for and the results of psychological climate perceptions. Their attempts included (1) determining assumptions underlying the phenomenon; (2) researching the psychological climate measurements; (3) testing for generalizability of psychological climate dimensions; (4) determining the roles of situational variables, person variables, and person by situation (PxS) interactions in perceptually/cognitive processes underlying psychological climate perceptions; and (5) investigating reciprocal causation between psychological climate (PC) perceptions and attitudes.

The extensive research conducted over the decades resulted in the provision of instruments and techniques to measure the assumed generalized climate dimensions. James and Sells found PC dimensions highly similar across a large number of samples, including US Navy enlisted personnel, production-line workers, supervisory and management personnel, fire fighters, system analysts, and computer programmers. There certainly is an absence of PC research conducted across samples of students at any level.

Further review of PC literature reveals that empirical research conducted has been limited to four types of organizations that represent distinct types of functions. Labeled according to Katz and Khan (1966), they are (1) Production/Maintenance organizations (PM), (2) Production (P), (3) Maintenance organization (M), and (4) Adaptive Maintenance organizations (A/M). Educational institutions do not fall into any of these categories; yet, PC dimensions have been generalized based on the assumed exhaustive research across sample types and organizational environments. The important question is whether the PC dimensions obtained from existing research can be reliably used to investigate psychological climates of student samples within educational organizations. Research in the area does not speak to this question.

A review of psychological climate research also reveals an absence of research of the role of ethnic heritage in the formation of the individual's psychological climate perceptions. James et al. (1978) and Schneider (1975) have concluded that position in organizations, levels of remuneration, role requirements, seniority, behavior of leaders, among other things, affect the PC perceptions experienced. The importance of culture/ethnicity as a determinant of perception has evidently been ignored in this field of research.

Psychological climate perception in the quest for diversity

Organizational leaders are investing inordinate amounts of time and money preparing their corporations and institutions of higher learning for increasing diversity. However, a significant amount of this effort is expended on providing information-based diversity training and including diversity issues into the college curriculum. Little effort is invested in addressing the fact that, as Thomas aptly puts it, "You can't grow peaches on an oak tree.... To grow peaches the roots must be peach friendly" (p. A-14). In other words, in order to successfully train organizational members to accept and respect diversity, these efforts must occur within an organization whose culture is diversity-friendly.

Despite this, most diversity efforts occur within organizations whose cultures endorse monoculturalism. Diversity experts ignore the salience of the organization's culture in the success of true organizational diversity. Consequently, they give little credence to the reality that attitudes toward human difference are developed through generations of psychological, social, and cultural conditioning. There seems to be not much concern that ethnically different organizational members may hold varying perceptions about human difference and will consequently hold varying attitudes toward diversity in the organization's climate. These attitudes may range from extremely positive to extremely negative.

Results in educational research seem to indicate differences among student racial subgroups in family characteristics, personality characteristics, experiences, levels of skills and abilities, characteristic modes of expressions and communication, and most importantly, ways of perceiving the world. These differences will perhaps influence their perception of human diversity, and as Hedegard and Brown (1969) speculate, may result in differences in reacting to and seeking out experiences and objects in the university environment. Previous studies (Willie and Levy, 1972), including those already mentioned, have compared climate-type variables for blacks and whites and suggest that people in different groups at the same university may function under different conditions and perceive the climate differently. The relationship between the organizational member's racial subgroups and his/her organizational climate perceptions is evident in educational research.

Although organizations place significant emphasis on diversity training, their diversity consultants and trainers usually neglect the salience of organizational members' perception in the success of their diversity efforts. They have not realized that they must focus on 'multiculturalizing' their organization if they are to influence organizational members' attitudes toward diversity. This is a process which requires strong, systemic efforts to create an organizational culture whose every fabric endorses and reinforces diversity and facilitates training. An important step therefore is not only to determine if different perceptions of organizational diversity exist between subracial groups within the organization but also to investigate differences based on ethnicity rather than race. They must subsequently determine those ethnic factors that do influence the perceptual differences. In other words, the study of psychological climate (PC) perceptions will be beneficial to investigations of climate perception differences among varied ethnic groups within organizations. This type of investigation is a necessary first step in any attempt at realigning university/college curriculum to meet the needs of the evolving multicultural corporate cultures. It will also prove valuable to those organizations committed to 'multiculturalizing' their systems.

This text posits that for those committed to creating an organizational culture that nourishes diversity, one of the critical steps is to identify the varying perceptions of the organization held by the different ethnic groups within the organization. It consequently analyzes the psychological climate perception construct, identifies its philosophical foundation, and investigates its influence on the perception of diversity in a university climate among African-American, Euro-American, and Latin-American college students at a predominantly Euro-American, private university in the United States.

The measurement of the psychological climate (PC) perceptions of ethnically different college students will determine those aspects of the college climate which are psychologically meaningful to those students. Results will indicate the influence of ethnicity as a variable in the development of psychological climate, a variable that has never been tested in investigations of psychological climate development. Part 1 of this text analyzes the two dominant theoretical constructs - perception and ethnicity- that define the relationship between ethnicity and the development of psychological climate perceptions. Part two details an experimental investigation of the psychological climate perceptions of organizational diversity issues among three ethnic groups of university students, and discussed the implications of the results for the quest for organizational diversity.

CHAPTER 2

Ethnicity and Psychological Climate Perception: A Conceptual and Philosophical Foundation

Unlike the psychological climate perception theory which has been precisely defined by its proponents, L.R. James, A. P. Jones, et al., ethnicity is an elusive phenomenon which has been defined and redefined by many scholars. The conceptualizations of this construct have evolved from a variety of paradigms embraced by researchers in various fields of study. Some, including Samovar and Porter (1991), see it as the results of the geographic origins of the minorities of a country. Others, such as Longstreet (1978), who embrace the phenomenological approach, suggest that ethnicity is a part of culture that is developed through direct contact with others (p. 22).

However despite the paradigm embraced, researchers, according to Schein (1990), must "not rush to measure things," until they are certain of exactly what they want to measure. Clarity in the operationalization of the two constructs - ethnicity and psychological climate perception - is critical since it will yield a theoretical and conceptual foundation which will allow for a holistic exploration of the relationship between ethnicity and psychological climate (pc) perceptions.

In approaching the challenge of investigating the relationship between organizational member's ethnicity and their perception of diversity in organizational climate, this chapter initially operationalizes the ethnicity and psychological climate perception constructs. It then advances a conceptual foundation and definitions of the contributing theories from which the experimental investigation proceeds. A philosophical understanding of an investigative research usually elucidates the theoretical phenomena involved in the investigation. In light of this, the final section of the chapter discusses the philosophical congruence between Symbolic Interactionism and Psychological Climate Perceptions theory.

Operational Definition of Theoretical Constructs

Ethnicity

This study embraces ethnicity as that part of an individual's cultural development that occurs prior to ages ten to twelve, the age at which, as Longstreet (1978) suggests, an individual reaches his/her full intellectual control. It is the result of the influence of family, scholastic, and national heritages on the individual before he/she achieves the age of full intellectual control. Samovar and Porter (1991) in *Communication Across Cultures* also suggest that ethnicity is usually the result of geographic origins of minorities of a country or culture and can be distinguished not by race but by the difference in backgrounds, perspectives, goals, and even language.

This study uses ethnicity to distinguish groups of students according to the geographic origins, language, social, and philosophical backgrounds of their families, and their own national and scholastic heritages. It also recognizes the difference in family, national, and scholastic ethnicity as proposed by Longstreet (1978).

Psychological climate (PC) perceptions

According to James and Sells (1981), psychological climate refers to "individuals' cognitive representations of proximal environments, expressed in terms that represent the personal or acquired meaning of environments to individuals" (p. 275). James, Hater, Gent, and Bruni (1978) formally define it as the individual's cognitive representations of relatively proximal situational events, expressed in terms that reflect the psychological meaning and significance of the situation to the individual.

Psychological climate, in this study, refers to the cognitive representations an individual uses to assign meaning to the situations or events he/she encounters in the environment. In essence, it is the individual's perception of situations/events that occur within his/her work environment that establishes a personal climate for him/her.

A Conceptual Framework

Psychological climate perceptions are a function of the individual's interaction with his/her environment (PxS). The individual is a product of his/her national, scholastic, and family ethnicity (Longstreet, 1978), which provides a cognitive structure that shapes his/her perception of the world. As individuals interact with their environment, they employ these cognitive constructions as they give psychological meaning to the situations or events encountered in the environment in which they function (James & Jones, 1974). This framework conceptualizes the relationship between ethnicity and the development of psychological climate perceptions. (See Figure 2.1)

Psychological climate (PC) perception theory

It has been recommended that psychological climate (PC) perception (a) reflects psychologically meaningful cognitive representations of situations rather than automatic reflections of specific situational events and, therefore, makes it an appropriate instrument for measuring ethnically inspired perceptions; (b) is generally more important than the objective situation in predicting many salient individual dependent variables; (c) is predicated on developmental experiences and frequently involves conflicting orientations generated by the preservation of valued and familiar schemas, on one hand, and openness to change in the interest of achieving adaptive and functional person-environment fits, on the other; and (d) is reciprocally related to memory, affect, and behavior in a causal model which predicts a reciprocal causation between perception and affect, and between individuals and environments (James et al., 1978).

This theory, derived from many areas of psychology, was developed by James and Jones (1974) to study individuals' perception of work environments. According to James and Sells (1981), "data from both field and experimental studies of climate perceptions suggest that individuals

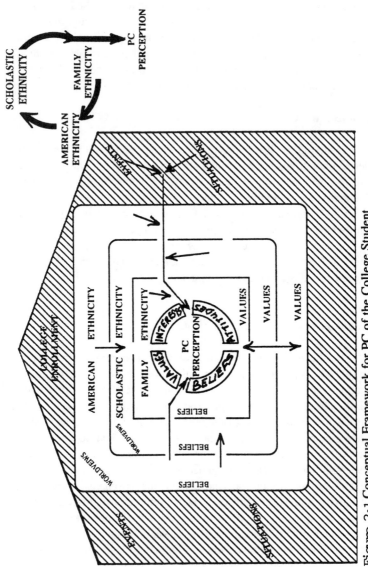

Figure 2:1 Conceptual Framework for PC of the College Student (PCCS).

in the same workgroup do not assign closely similar meaning to their work environments" (p.284). Reasons advanced for this lack of perceptual agreement focused on differences in information processing and idiosyncrasies in perceptual/cognitive filtering and interpretations. James et al. (1978) explain that each employee/member in an organization, through a process of cognitive constructions, will inevitably interpret situations or events in ways that are psychologically meaningful to him/her.

Interestingly, PC uses the individual as the unit of analysis. It offers the opportunity to analyze the perceptions of each member in relation to the organization as determined by his/her cognitive representation of relatively proximal situational events expressed in a manner that reflects the psychological meaning and significance of the situation/event to him/her. This means, according to Ekehammar (1974), that "psychological environments may be different for different individuals" (p. 1034).

Psychological climate (PC) theory measures allow for the measurement of individual differences in perceptions that reflect the psychological meaning and significance of the college environment to ethnically different students. This study embraces the notion that the college environment perception is a function of the person by situation (PxS) interaction. The student employs a set of cognitive constructs as he/she perceives the college environment. However, according to theories of perception as advanced by numerous scholars including Samovar and Porter (1991, Triandis and Albert (1987), and Verderber (1987), our perception of the world is culturally inspired. According to Samovar and Porter (1991) in *Communication Between Cultures,* "culture determines our view of the world, and each culture perceives a different reality. This is because people need to make observations and gather knowledge that make sense within their particular cultural perspective" (p.116).

The ethnicity vs. culture hypothesis

This study endorses the general consensus that culture is a set of beliefs and expectations about how people cognize and organize their lives. However, in its attempt to construct a broad theoretical framework from which to operate, this study embraces a hypothesis advanced by Longstreet (1978) which explains the dynamics of the development of ethnicity as an aspect of cultural development.

Longstreet (1978) makes a distinction between culture and ethnicity as she views culture as " whatever people do to nature; what is not 'natural' is 'cultural'" (p. 18). This author posits that everyone has a cultural capacity; that is, they are capable of creating what is not present in nature, they can imitate their peers, and they can manipulate or adapt to environmental situations. In essence, the properties that constitute culture are the traits that result from circumstances or the limitation of circumstances. It can be a universal phenomenon such as the culture of poverty. Poor people throughout the world seem to follow identifiably similar patterns because they do not have the means to do otherwise. Culture consequently can be defined as the network of responses to the interaction between people and the circumstances they share. Longstreet writes:

> Ethnicity is that portion of cultural development that occurs before the individual is in complete command of his/her abstract intellectual powers and that is formed primarily through the individual's early contact with family, neighbors, friends, and others, as well as with his/her immediate environment of the home and neighborhood. (p.19)

According to Longstreet, the human being does not develop abstract thinking powers until somewhere between the ages of ten and twelve. Prior to this stage, children have limited capacity to judge the ways of behavior that they are absorbing. They acquire early cultural traits at a time when they are not in full command of their intellectual powers. Even though the individual develops an intellectual control over his/her ethnically learned behaviors, this control is never complete since a significant portion of what is learned ethnically occurs at a very low awareness level. It is almost impossible to be able to modify ethnic traits absorbed as children. Longstreet supports this fact by saying, "We cannot, intellectually or emotionally, change the multitude of traits that would have to be altered to change our basic ethnicity (p. 20).

Ethnicity is developed through direct contacts with others and the immediate environment. Longstreet (1978) has emphasized the importance of "roles" that have been ethnically learned and posits that actions required by roles that are learned early in cultural development may be impervious to change. She makes a distinction between "scholastic" and "American" ethnicity but suggests that they also are both learned during the early phases of cultural development. She writes: "learning to be a student has many of the characteristics of learning to be a member of an ethnic group" (p. 22). Therefore, a whole way of living is assimilated from one's family life and school life in those early stages of cultural development.

The traits of scholastic ethnicity have a national sphere of influence and could be a part of the American ethnicity. Different ethnic groups share in an American culture as they must react to similar phenomena; these reactions are learned in the early cultural development stages. It is clear to see why Longstreet (1978) hypothesizes that "while there are significant ethnic differences among American blacks and other American ethnic groups, American blacks are culturally closer to these groups than to the blacks of Ethiopia or Nigeria" (p.25).

Samovar and Porter (1991) in *Communication Between Cultures* see ethnicity as the results of geographic origins of the minorities of a country or culture. For example, Cubans living in Florida and Mexicans living in California might be citizens of the United States, yet the dominant culture does not consider them part of the majority culture. According to these scholars, there are similar situations in Canada where there are English-Canadians and French-Canadians. They belong to the same race and are both citizens of Canada but maintain different backgrounds, perspectives, goals, and language.

Using Lonstreet's hypothesis, this study then speculates that Latin-American, African-American, and Euro-American college students in any American college can be expected to be bearers of their family's ethnic heritage as well as an American heritage, and a national scholastic heritage to a large extent. Even though there are some who may be citizens of the United States, they do not belong to the same race, do not share similar ethnic family heritages and, in the case of Latin-Americans, do not share similar language backgrounds. Surely, they will also differ as a result of the differences in their intellectual powers, but as Longstreet (1978) suggests, because of early cultural developments of their family, scholastic, and national ethnicities, significant aspects of their tri-cultural being will be impervious to change.

It is consequent that American college student will share a scholastic and national culture but will differ culturally as a result of family ethnicity (See Figure 2.2). This study expects that any differences in cultural attributes among college students will result in equal differences in their cognitive processes. This factor in turn impacts on their perceptions of situations or events within the college environment, resulting in a differing in perception among ethnically different students in the college.

The relationship between culture and perception

Samover and Porter (1991) in *Intercultural Communication* assert that there is cultural diversity in perception which provides humankind with alternative views of reality. Perception is the manner in which we make sense of our environments. Stotland and Canon (1972), Verderber

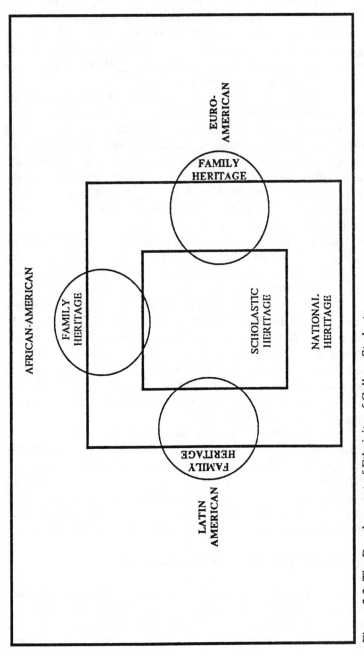

Figure 2.2: The Development of Ethnicity of College Students

(1986), and Triandis and Albert (1987) are among many scholars who have advanced theories of the perception process. The consensus, however, as restated by Samovar and Porter (1991) in *Communication Across Cultures* is that perception is the process by which an individual selects, evaluates, and organizes stimuli from the external environment.

The physical perception process is the same in all people, but there is variation within each step influenced by variations in culture. The first stage is identification or recognition, which occurs through a configuration of sound or light waves that impinge on our senses and are transmitted through our nerves. This process, according to Samovar and Porter, happens in very much the same way for everyone. However, the second stage, which involves interpreting and evaluating these light or sound waves, is not the same for all people. This step is a learned process influenced primarily by culture" (p.104).

Culture is important to our perceptions of the world. Interpretations of what has been identified are individualistic and represent unique sets of experiences in the culture in which the individual has been raised. " By observing the way people around us behave, we learn how to interpret the world," write Samovar and Porter in *Communication Across Cultures,* (p.104). It is through these learning processes, the capacity for the identifying of and giving meaning and value to social objects and events is developed. In other word, we learn to perceive our environment within the culture in which we are raised.

This study recognizes that culture allows a large group of people to have similar experiences. For example, all American college students would have been exposed to the "American ethnicity" and to a "scholastic ethnicity" as suggested by Longstreet (1978). This does not mean that all students within an American college are the same. There is diversity in family ethnicity, in some cases, diversity in American, scholastic, and family ethnicity as represented by students who have immigrated to the United States during their college years.

This study examines the implications of variations in ethnicity for variations in psychological climate perceptions of college environments among college students based on these theories that posit a relationship between perception and culture.

Symbolic Interactionism: A Philosophical Foundation for Psychological Climate (PC) Theory

Psychological Climate (PC) theory postulates that the organizational member's work environment is his/her own subjective world perceived in terms of his/her personal meaning. The factor that influences that member's behavior is the perception that he/she assigns to situation/events that occur within the environment as he/she responds to cognitive representations of the organizational situations/events. It is defined as " a set of perceptions that reflect how work environments, including organizational attributes, are cognitively appraised and represented in terms of their meaning to and significance for individuals" (James et al., 1988). In other words, this paradigm is based on the philosophy that giving meaning to environmental attributes requires processes that produce cognitive interpretations of significance to the individual. According to James et al. (1988), Ekehammer (1974), and Endler and Magnusson (1976) suggest that "these processes take place within the individual and involve interactions between environmental stimuli and personalistic attributes such as values and expectations" (p.129). The psychological climate theory is rooted in the philosophy that dynamic social interactions are causes of meaning, and meaning is a psychological variable.

The theory of symbolic interactionism gives credence to the Psychological Climate (PC) theory as it is grounded in the position that the world is a subjective one. This theory, like the psychological climate theory, defines the environment from the individual's perspective and is concerned with its psychological descriptions or its perceived meaning.

This study embraces the postulations of PC theory as it wholeheartedly endorses the philosophy of symbolic interactionism of the environment. Grounded in this doctrine, the current research investigates the very source from which symbolic interactionism operates to provide the organizational member with a cognitive process for perceiving his/her environment. The current research is aware of the cognitive processes that shape perception and is concerned with the student and how he/she perceives his/her university environment. More importantly, it is concerned with the factors/cues in the environment that are salient to the formation of the individual's views/perception of the environment (psychological climate).

The origins of symbolic interactionism

Jessor (1981) quotes Bridgman, the father of operationism, as saying that "a proper appreciation of (first-person report) will alter the common picture of science as something essentially public into something essentially private" (p.296). There has been an evolutionary shift from thinking about the environment as objective to the coming to terms with its subjective nature. Also, according to Jessor, concern for the subjective has underlain sociological and psychological thinking as far back as the primary symbolic interactionists: Charles Cooley, John Dewey, I.A. Thomas, and George Herbert Mead. It has also long been the preoccupation of the symbolic interactionists —Blumer, Rose, and Wilson— who argued that "the environment of action is, in the last analysis, constituted by the actor" (Jessor, 1981, p. 298). The classical environment concept in this perspective is the definition of the situation. In essence, reality is what the individual defines it to be.

According to Jessor (1981), in the field of psychology there was the renewal of interest in the inner experience as legitimate psychological data. In Lewinian field theory, this perspective led to an insistence in describing the environment as it is perceived or experienced by the actor. Classical interactionism theoretical formulations emerged from this concern with the environment from the actor's perspective, that is, concern with its psychological description or its perceived meaning.

Contemporary social behavior formulations include Bandura's (1978) acknowledgments that "the environment is partly of a person's own making," (p.345) and "external influences operate largely through cognitive processes" (p.355). Essentially, the cognitive and perceptual concepts proposed by recent interactionists have the same foundations as the classical interactionists' psychological environment. This perspective emphasizes the individual's psychological representations and his/her construction of the environment.

The multiplicity of environments

Human action takes place in multiple environments simultaneously. Action can be viewed in a physical, geographic, cultural, social, structural, or psychological context, depending on the conceptual orientation of a particular discipline, the explanatory objectives of a particular researcher, or the guiding purpose of a particular actor. This multiplicity is what makes understanding the environment problematic in research. Jessor (1981) proposed three principles for organizing the multiplicity and diversity of environments in relation to the disciplinary goal of achieving psychological explanation. The principles are (1) Environment-Behavior Mediation, (2) Experiential Proximity of Environments and (3) Invariance of Behavior with perceived environment.

This study focuses on individual's action within a cultural or psychological context as they function within their organizations. It embraces the principle of Experiential Proximity of environments as it seeks to analyze how college students construct their environment. The Experiential Proximity of Environments is a principle which postulates that "the multiple and various environments can be ordered along a dimension of conceptual proximity to experience, perception, interpretation or to psychological response" (Jessor, 1981, p. 300). The "distal" end of the dimension signifies the environments that are relatively remote from direct experience and are without specific functional significance for the person. They are environments of physics, geography, biology, and institutional sociology.

The "proximal" end of the dimension constitutes environments that are closer to being directly perceived and experienced; they have rather direct implications for perception and meaning. Jessor further states: "Along the distal-proximal dimension, the most proximal environment would be perceived environment, the environment of immediate significance for the actor" (p. 300). In other words, the psychological environment is most proximal. In this case, the proximal environment is the organization experience; therefore the situation and events which occur within the organization have implications for perception and meaning.

CHAPTER 3

How Ethnicity Influences Psychological Climate Perceptions: Theoretical Perspectives

To understand the relationship between organizational members' ethnicity and their psychological climate (PC) perceptions of diversity within their organization demands a comprehensive exploration of all the theoretical constructs that contribute to this phenomenon. However, before embarking on any experimental investigations in this area, researchers will benefit from an understanding of the past and existing organizational climates within which they are conducting their research. A study of the organization may illuminate key variables that influence the outcome of research findings.

Consequently, as this chapter analyzes the relationship between ethnicity/culture and the development of psychological perceptions, it begins by reviewing studies of climate in university environments and also takes a look at the shift in perceptual trends of university students throughout the years. It then provides a comprehensive review of empirical literature that addresses the development of ethnicity and the formation of psychological climate perceptions. It in turn discusses the relationship between ethnicity and perception. Central to this review is the portion of this chapter that readdresses the philosophical congruence between Symbolic Interaction and Psychological Climate theories as it examines the psychological climate constructs, cognitive social learning, and interactional psychology theories from a symbolic interaction perspective.

The Study of University Climate

Pfeifer (1976) states that "organizational climate has traditionally been viewed as a characteristic of the organization and not a measure of individual differences among people" (p. 342). Studies in university climate however have used climate as a characteristic of individuals as they attempt to test for variances within and between groups in specific criteria in the university environment (Pfeifer & Schneider, 1974; Pfeifer, 1976; Centra & Rock, 1971; Hedegard & Brown, 1969; Willie & Levy, 1972).

The dynamics that underlie academic performance of university students have been attributed to university climate. Astin (1968), Centra and Rock (1971), and Rock et al. (1970) have examined the relationship between student performance and university climate as measured by scores on the Graduate Record Examination (GRE) test. Yet other studies have shown that a high university dropout rate may be attributed to the incompatibility of students and university climate (Patton, 1955; Funkenstein, 1962; Pervin, 1967).

Although there has been a number of studies investigating the university environment and more specifically interinstitution comparisons among college environments (Astin & Holland, 1961; Stern, 1962), the efforts expended on understanding the differences in perceptions of university climate among ethnically/racially/culturally different students in the university are limited. However, the existing research that investigates perceptual differences between black and white students within the same university environment concludes that people in different groups at the same university may function under different conditions and perceive the climate differently (Pfeifer & Schneider, 1974).

Hedegard and Brown (1969) alluded to the importance of understanding students' perceptions of the university climate on finding modal Negro-white differences in experiences, levels of skills and abilities, characteristic modes of expression and communication, and ways of viewing the world. They suggest that these differences would result in "differences in reacting to and seeking out experiences and objects in the environment" (p.143). Willie and Levy (1972) noted a separatism between black and white students in the same environment which they also thought could lead to different university-related experiences.

Investigations into the differences in black and white student perceptions of university climate conducted by Pfeifer and Schneider (1974) found consistent and significant differences on two factor scales between blacks and whites, with blacks perceiving the university climate more negatively. One out of the five factors extracted for whites was racism, while two factors out of the six extracted for blacks were racism.

In keeping with these findings, Pfeifer (1976) reasoned that "since climate can have effects on performance, it is a variable that should not be overlooked when considering racial bias in the academic setting" (p.341). He consequently embarked on an investigation of the relationship between scholastic aptitude, perception of university climate, and college success for black and white students. He correlated university climate and Scholastic Aptitude Test (SAT) scores with two criteria of academic success, grade point average (GPA), and students' estimated probability of receiving a degree in racial subgroups. He found that SAT scores were significantly related to GPA in both samples and not related to students' estimated probability of receiving a degree in either racial groups. However, a positive university climate perception was associated with high criterion scores for whites, while it was associated with a low criterion scores for blacks. The significant correlation of GPA with estimated probability of receiving a degree in both samples was even more significant in the black sample.

A Shift in Perceptual Trends of University Students

It is interesting to note that in a longitudinal study, Goodwin (1982) found that students' perceptions of the university climate change over the four years of undergraduate education. Using the College and University Environment Scales (CUES), her study examined 408 undergraduates after four, 10, and 14 years out of college. Findings indicate that freshmen intensified the strength of their perceptions concerning academic excellence after four years of college. Students' perceptions after a decade showed a time lag occurring but indicated a gradual change. Of crucial concern to the field of climate research in higher learning is that trends findings show a shift back to conservatism of an earlier era. The major exception was a renewed interest in scholarship.

The conclusions of this study highlights the dynamic nature of college environments, which seemingly are a function of the ideological trends of the nation within which they exist. The question of the generalizability of the conclusions of the studies in differences in psychological climate perceptions of culturally different university students throughout time is of crucial concern. The social forces that operate in the broader atmospheres of the research settings will certainly impact the enculturation process and inevitably the perceptions of university students of all ethnicities/cultures.

A review of the literature that examines university climate perceptions among black and white students reveals a trend of the perceptual experiences of the different groups moving from relatively divergent in the 1970s (Hegegard and Brown,1974; Kegan, 1978; Kitano, 1974) to the same groups sharing relatively similar perceptions of campus ambience and institutional policies, and having similar academic and career goals (Astin, 1982; Cheatham et al., 1984). According to Cheatham (1986), there is evidence that blacks are generally satisfied with the academic quality and prestige of white institutions, although they recognize the high psychic costs as "quid pro quo" (Fleming, 1984; Patterson et al.,1984).

Taylor (1986a) is more embittered by the apparent new profile of the black students on predominantly white campuses in the 1980s. He has come to terms with the fact that "things have changed and black students have also changed" (p. 196), but he experiences difficulty in the accepting of the changes specifically in attitudes, perceptions, and expectations of today's black student on predominantly white college campuses. He advances a controversial profile of the black student of the 1980s using Frederick Harper's (1969) article entitled "Black Student Revolt on the White Campus" as a basis for updating the perception of what "being black" means to the majority of black students on predominantly white campuses in the 1980s.

Taylor's profile characterizes the black student of the 1980s as being ashamed to interact with students of his own race, not understanding the significance of African history or African-American studies, believing that the white faculty and administration understand his problems, being very comfortable in his white surroundings, not seeing the need to join any black student organizations on campus, not understanding why he got a "B" when he deserved an "A", and talking less of being black so that he can easily become part of the group of white friends.

The response to his profile was profound (Cheatham, 1986; Cuyjet, 1986; Wright, 1986). Cheatham (1986) describes Taylor's profile as "provocative" and considers it to be " a disturbing caricature of the 1980s version of that student and that environment." He continues:

Taylor's version seems an indictment that lacks sufficient
attention to the social processes related to the integration of
blacks in American society. In fact, his conclusion is
reminiscent of Frazier's (1957) refutation of Herskovitz's (1941)
contention that black Americans had lost their sense of
history and heritage. (p.202)

Cheatham concludes that it is important to have an understanding of
the current environments. This understanding will come through meticu-
lous analysis and comprehension of social forces. Cuyjet (1986) also views
Taylor's representation of today's black student as clearly one-sided in
depicting only one kind of black student : "To offer such a picture without broadening it to represent the multidimensions of today's black students," he says, "would be a serious injustice" (p.204). Cujet further states:

Black students have, indeed, changed since the 1960s. Given
the changes in the world, the country,   our college and
university campuses and the Black community itself, they would
be pathetically anachronistic if they had not changed. Part of
this change is caused by the assimilation that Taylor describes.
He owes it to the Black students, however, to allow that there is
some benefit to this lack of anxiety about being in a White
environment. As many students of the 1960s can attest, it is hard
to attend to your studies when you are angry all the time...Taylor
seems to believe that Black students lack the capacity to retain
their own culture while experiencing and learning from another.
This is a grave disservice to the abilities of many students.
(p.205)

Wright (1986) believes that Taylor has confused "students" definition of ethnic identity with their reactions to environmental stresses. She
challenges his assertion that hearing derogatory comments about black
people from white teachers and not challenging them is not a definition
of "blackness" but an illustration of a students' reaction to a unique environmental stress (perceived racism on campus). She believes that Taylor
does not adequately distinguish between "a definition of being black and
negative reactions to environmental stresses." This confusion, she believes, contributes to a misrepresentation of black students and their ethnic identity (p.206).

The current study recognizes the credence of the diverse philosophies that underlie each view of the phenomenon. It also realizes that

these divergent views may be shaped by the social forces that are in existence within the respective environments from which the respective authors write. The salience of racism and its by-products differs from state to state. Taylor writes from his office as the Dean of students office at Loyola University in Chicago; Cheatham writes from the Pennsylvania State University; Cuyjet writes from Northern Illinois University; and Wright writes from the University of Texas at Austin.

Very little research has investigated the variance of perceptions within ethnic/racial groups of university students. However, one such study (Babbit & Burbash, 1979) compared the perceptions of social control among 180 black students randomly selected from a large urban university, a medium-sized urban college, and a small urban center, all in a metropolitan area in the state of New York. They found that Urban-center blacks viewed the school's authority structure in a significantly more positive light than did university and college blacks. The absence of investigation of perceptual climate differences within groups of ethnically different university students perpetuates the lack of understanding of the independent variables that influence the formation of psychological climate.

Summary of the study of university climate

The current study embraces the conclusions of the body of research that suggests that in general black and white students do tend to share similar perceptions of overall university climate. It also recognizes that perceptions of certain dimensions of university climate do on occasions differ for black students and white students. However, the review of literature in the area has revealed an absence of investigations into the climate perceptions of Latin American students who attend the same university/college as blacks and whites. It also reveals a lack of studies investigating variance in climate perceptions within groups of students of the same race or ethnicity.

Some researchers have alluded to the fact that it is more often difficult for black and Hispanic students than non-minority students to adjust academically and socially on predominantly white campuses (Fleming,1984; Garza & Nelson, 1973; Gibbs, 1973; Pruitt, 1970). This finding suggests a similarity of experiences of black and Hispanic students on predominantly white campuses.

Research also does not address the actual ways in which the different ethnic groups of students use the cues in the university environment to formulate their perceptions of the climate. More specifically, this research sees the need to identify the dimensions of the university climate that are of particular salience to the different ethnic groups of student in the university. In essence, it is important to determine those dimensions of psychological climate of university students that differ; after all, the dimensions that are psychologically meaningful to the student are the ones that he/she will employ to formulate his/her perception of the university environment. The psychological climate paradigm allows for the measurement and identification of salient dimensions of climate perceptions.

The Development of Psychological Climate Perception Theory

Climate researchers in organizational studies have realized the subjective nature of the environment and have also made that shift from thinking of the work environment as objective or as a set of organizational attributes to embracing it as perceptual and as an individual attribute rather subjective in nature. Organizational climate research has experienced major ideological shifts throughout the decades, the major one being the evolution from the objective to the subjective.

James et al. (1978) formally define psychological climate (PC) perception as the individual's cognitive representations of relatively proximal events, expressed in terms that reflect the psychological meaning and significance of the situation to the individual. Psychological climate (PC) perception represents the perceptions that an individual forms from situations or events in his/her environment that are psychologically meaningful to him/her. The individual in psychological climate research becomes the unit of analysis.

The evolution of climate research: the controversy

Organizational climate research has carved out a prominent place in the history of organizational studies. It occupies a popular and glorious position in organizational and industrial psychology. For almost twenty-five years, this research has yielded diverse and contradictory results as concern increased, not only for the psychological environment, but also for social, organizational, and situational influences on behavior. A resultant conceptual morass grew out of attempts to understand the phenomenon.

A review of the literature and studies in the field will reveal a diversity of conceptual and operational definitions and measurement techniques regarding organizational climate. Guion (1973) attributed this "climate controversy" to the evident inconsistencies among units of theory, observation, and analysis (Glick, 1985). The appropriate units of theory in climate research have been debated for almost two decades (Guion, 1973; Hellriegel & Slocum. 1974; James, 1982; James & Jones, 1974; Powell & Butterfield, 1978; Glick, 1985).

One major source of dispute is the conceptualization of organizational climate (OC). One school of thought views OC as the aggregation of PC scores. Scholars who embrace this —James and Jones (1974); James and Sells (1981); Joyce and Slocum (1979) and James et al.(1988)— believe that "if individuals in an organization share perceptions on a PC dimension such as conflict and ambiguity, then it is possible to aggregate the PC scores because perceptual agreement implies a shared assignment of meaning" (James, 1988, p. 129). The opposing school of thought rejects this conceptualization of OC. Glick (1985), for example, suggests that OC is a "result of sociological/organizational processes" (p. 605). He posits that OC should be conceptualized as an organizational phenomenon and not as an aggregate of PC. He defines it as "a generic term for a broad class of organizational, rather than psychological, variables that describe the organizational context for individuals' actions" (Glick,1985, p. 613).

James and Jones (1974) attempted to review the major theoretical concerns and relevant research related to climate in industrial or business organizations. Their review identified three separate but not mutually exclusive approaches to defining and measuring organizational climate. They distinguished these approaches as (1) the "multiple measurement organizational attribute approach," which regards the organizational climate exclusively as a set of organizational attributes or main effects measurable by a variety of methods; (2) the "perceptual measurement-organizational attribute approach," which views organizational climate as a set of perceptual variables which are still seen as organizational main effects; and (3) "the perceptual measurement-individual approach," which sees organizational climate as perceptual and as an individual attribute (James & Jones, 1974, p. 1096).

Psychological climate theory

James and Jones are two of the scholars who attempted to make the distinction between climate regarded as an organizational attribute and climate regarded as an individual attribute. They contradicted the initial attempts to consider the organization as the natural unit of theory in organizational climate research as conducted by Argyris (1957); Forehand and Gilmer (1964) and Litwin and Stringer (1968). James and Jones subsequently made a distinction between "psychological" and "organizational" climate and suggested that different units of theory (individual and organizational) are appropriate for the two constructs. The term "organizational climate" must be maintained when climate is viewed from an organizational perspective. However, when viewed as an individual attribute, the use of the term "psychological climate," is recommended (James & Jones, 1974). Consequently, the "perceptual measurement-individual attribute" approach must assume the term "psychological climate" which is so called because of the emphasis placed on the intervening psychological processes in the individual attribute approach.

Multiple units of theory should be recognized in climate research mainly because psychological, subunit (groups), and organizational climates may differ empirically. If there were only one unit of theory in climate research, then there would be no reason to adopt different labels for organizational, subunit, and psychological climate. According to Glick (1985), "Organizational climate connotes an organizational unit of theory, it does not refer to the climate of an individual, workgroup, occupation, department, or job" (p.602). Researchers interested in other types of climate should, according to Howe (1977), adopt appropriate labels and units of theory and analysis.

The Role of other Theories and their Assumptions for Psychological Climate

A major advantage of differentiating between organizational and psychological climate is the additional clarity permitted in both the definition and measurement of climate. Psychological climate provides a movement toward formulating specific theoretical statements regarding the nature of the intervening psychological processes between the organizational situation and the attributes and behavior of individual members of the organization (James & Jones, 1974).

Psychological climate has been the center of conceptual and empirical attentions throughout the years, but there has been a simultaneous neglect of investigations into the specific influences on the development of climate perception. Ornstein (1986) claims that conceptually, various perceptual processes have been proposed to account for the development of individual's perceptions of climate. Cognitive social learning theory and interactional psychology, according to James, Hater, Gent, and Bruni (1978), are two such theories that are particularly relevant to a study of this type.

The attempt to integrate postulates of PC theory with basic perception and cognition, environmental psychology (Ittelson et al.,1974) and social learning and cognitive social learning theory (Bandura, 1978; Mahoney, 1977; Mischel, 1973; Stotland & Canon, 1972) have been endorsed by James et al. (1978). Major emphasis was placed on the implications of these theoretical models for PC. These scholars posit that, among other things, PC (a) reflects psychologically meaningful, cognitive representations of situations rather that automatic reflections of specific situational events; (b) is generally more important than the objective situation in predicting many salient individual dependent variables; (c) is predicated on developmental experience and frequently involves conflicting orientations generated by the preservation of valued or familiar schemas, on one hand, and the need for adaptation to the situation on the other, (d) is related reciprocally to memory, affect , and behavior in a causal model which predicts a reciprocal causation between perception and affect, and between individuals and environments.

The social learning and cognitive social learning theory when used in PC research allows for the minor reconceptualization of the phenomenon based on a psychological-cognitive framework. It suggests that individuals first become aware of stimuli in the environment and then become aware of the meaning that is evoked in their minds as a result of the stimuli. The meanings are cognitively processed by the perceiver who consequently uses this information in forming cognitive schemas of the organization.

Assumptions gleaned from this psychological-cognitive perspective have been advanced by James et al. (1978) and by James & Sells, (1981). The assumptions are as follows: (1) PC perceptions reflect the psychological meaning and significance of the situation to the individual; (2) It represents a perceptually based, psychologically processed description of the situation/environment. In other words, the situation that a person "knows" is a product of cognitive constructions (e.g., cognitive maps) which involves various forms of Person by Situation (PxS) interactions (James & Jones, 1974; Schneider, 1975; James et al. 1978) or symbolic interactions. This processing results in cognitive representations or interpretations that reflect the psychological meaning of the work environment/situation to the individual, for example, the extent of openness or warmth the individual perceives in the work environment.

Cognitive social learning theory and interactional psychology:-
Implications for PC

James et al. (1978) employed four fundamentals of cognitive-learning theory and interactional psychology as summarized by Mahoney
(1977) when analyzing their implications for PC. This study concentrates
on three of the four advanced fundamentals. Fundamental #1 claims that
"individuals respond primarily to cognitive representations of situations
rather than situations per se;" Fundamental #2 posits that these cognitive
representations of situations are related to prior experiences and learning;
and Fundamental #3 claims that most human learning is cognitively mediated. These theories provide a basis for understanding the psychological climate phenomenon in organizations. This research analyzes the
fundamentals of these theories as it questions the basis for the development of cognitive representations.

Fundamental #1 claims "individuals respond primarily to cognitive
representations of situations rather than situations per se." Ekehammer
(1974) defines the psychological environment as the subjective world,
which "reflects the individual's perceptions and constructions of the external environment and can be described in terms of psychological variables" (p.1027). Consequently, it can be concluded that individuals perceive situations in terms of their personal meaning; a fusion of current
interactional and cognitive theories. Endler and Magnusson (1976) further noted that the factor that most influences an individual's behavior is
the perception he/she assigns to a situation. Bowers (1973) and Argyle
and Little (1972) reflect that individuals perceive the same situation differently so that psychological environments may be different for different individuals. According to James et al. (1978), the consequent conclusions are that " (a) individuals respond primarily to cognitive representations of the situation; (b) cognitive representations can be described in
terms that are psychologically meaningful; and (c) cognitive representations of the same situation may differ among individuals" (p.787).

This study posits that this fundamental of the cognitive learning theory
provides a basis for the assumption that individuals who are in the same
workgroup may not assign closely similar meanings to their environments.
James et. al (1978) and Schneider (1975) have advanced a number of
potential reasons for the probable lack of perceptual agreement. These
reasons ranged from individual differences in information processing and
idiosyncrasies in perceptual/cognitive filtering and interpretations to the
likelihood that individuals in the same work environment might not be
exposed to the same set of situational attributes and events.

James and Sells (1981) have posited other reasons for variance in meanings of work environment. These reasons include, (1) individuals may have different role requirements, (2) they may perform different job functions, (3) they may be recipients of different leader behavior, (4) they may have different social relationships with other work group members, and (5) they may receive different levels of pay as a function of merit or seniority.

An important postulate of the cognitive learning theory as advanced in Fundamental #1 claims that individuals respond to cognitive representations of situations and consequently perceive organizational situations in terms of their own personal meaning. This research questions the very source of cognitive representations from where meaning is formed. It becomes important to understand what shapes the cognitive process of individuals. Fundamental #2 speaks to this question.

Fundamental #2 claims that cognitive representations of situations are related to prior experiences and learning. It posits that most learning is cognitively mediated. James et al. (1978) have made important obser-' vations of the cognitive social learning theory and cognition based on a considerable number of reports. These observations suggest the following: (1) Perception, learning, and memory are interrelated cognitive processes; perception, the scholars suggest, is intrinsically tied to learning and memory; (2) perceptions of a particular situation are based on learned cognitive schemas developed for purposes of organization or interpretations; they are a partial function of the ability to recall schemas for interpretive purposes; (3) individuals who have had different learning experiences develop different cognitive schemas to interpret situations; (4) cognitive schemas, especially Higher Order Schemas (HOSs) are resistant to change because they are abstract and generalized and are influenced by inconsistencies between existing HOSs and specific situation stimuli in particular situations; they are also familiar and valued and (5) there is an antinomy between the desire to preserve familiar and valued cognitive schemas and the degree to which cognitive schemas are open to change. These observations suggest that individuals who are ethnically and culturally different will perceive their organizational environment in different ways.

James et al. (1978) have suggested that "perceptions of the same situation are likely to differ among individuals and the reasons for these differences are psychologically important" (p.795). They have noted the tendency in PC research to ignore the bases for individual differences in climate perceptions. They believe the reasons are that (1) climate research has continually viewed climate as a situational attribute rather than an individual attribute; consequently, difference in perceptions among persons, groups, roles, and jobs have been viewed as error variance; and (2) climate research tended to emphasize an historical view regarding the formulation of climate perceptions since perceptions were presumed to be accommodative or functional. Perceptions were thought to bend to the need for the development of an adaptive person-situation fit for each new situation.

Summary of the development of psychological climate theory

Climate theory has been the source of theoretical concern and controversy through the years. The construct has been debated for decades and is still the source of debate today. However, in the 1970s James and Jones made a breakthrough in this theoretical twist as they suggested that the foundation of the problem is the absence of various units of analysis in investigation procedures. Investigators, they say, must know the unit of analysis being studied and employ the relevant measures.

Psychological climate was proposed as a construct which measures the individual as opposed to the department or organization as a whole. Psychological climate theory is concerned with the individual who perceives situations/events in his/her environment in accordance with what is significant or meaningful to him/her. This review includes an analysis of the role of the cognitive social learning and interactional psychology theories in the understanding of the psychological climate theories. However, although it focuses on the cognitive process that determines perception, it neglects to include the influence of culture on that process.

The current study suggests that variations in cultural conditioning is the basis for individual differences in climate perception in organizations. However, the study focuses on analyzing the complexity of the cognitive perceptual process as explained by scholars such as Stotland and Canon (1972), Verderber (1987), Triandis and Albert (1987), Samovar and Porter (1991) as it seeks to determine the basis for individual differences in this cognitive processing or interpretation of stimuli.

Theories of Perception Development

Perception is the internal process by which we select, evaluate, and organize stimuli from the external environment, according to Samovar & Porter (1991) in *Intercultural Communication.* This means that perception is the conversion of the physical energies of our environment into meaningful experiences. Samover and Porter make a distinction between perception and social perception, which they consider to be "the process by which we construct our unique realities by attributing meaning to the social objects and events we encounter in our environments" (p. 14).

Verderber (1987) defines perception as "the process of gathering sensory information and assigning meaning to it" (p.26). The eyes, nose, ears, skin, and taste buds collect the information from which the brain selects. It then organizes, interprets, and finally evaluates the information. The result is perception.

The process of perception occurs in three stages: (1) selection of stimuli, (2) organization of stimuli, and (3) interpretation of stimuli. These three stages occur almost simultaneously (Verderber, 1987). Selections are made on the basis of interest, need and expectation. According to Gestalt psychologists, organization follows rules of (a) simplicity, the tendency to simplify relatively complex perceptions into some recognizable form; (b) pattern, the tendency to look at sets of shapes and tend to group them along common lines; (c) proximity, the tendency to group things that are physically close together; and (d) good form. If perception has a gap, we will most likely see it as a closed figure. Interpretation is the process of explaining what has been selected and organized; it gives an evaluation.

Samovar and Porter (1991) offer a similar theory of the perceptual process. They explain:

> The physical process of perception is pretty much the same in all people. We have sensory organs such as eyes, ears and noses that permit us to sense our environment. These sensations are routed through our nervous system to our brains, where the sensations are interpreted and endowed with meaning in a two-stage sequence. The first stage is recognition or identification, in which configuration of light or sound waves is identified as perhaps a car or music. The second stage involves the interpretation and evaluation of that which has been identified. The result of that last step, however, is not the same in all people. This step is a learned process influenced by culture. (p. 104)

These authors have employed different terms to explain the same process posited by Verderber (1987). In essence, the brain selects incoming information, organizes it into an identifiable pattern, and then interprets/evaluates it.

A review of the literature that addresses the development of perception suggests a similar developmental process. Stotland and Canon (1972)

developed a model which was based on research and theoretical proposi-
tions regarding cognitive processing models. The model is generally consistent with more recent models of perceptual and cognitive information
processing (Triandis & Albert, 1987; Verderber, 1987; Samovar & Porter,
1991).

The schema theory

The Schema theory is a theoretical paradigm that has been developed from cognitive social learning theory. This paradigm describes how
individuals might represent situations cognitively. Stotland and Canon
(1972) advanced a hierarchical model to describe the development of
cognitive schemas. The concepts are (a) dimensions, (b) lower-order
schemas (LOs) and (c) higher-order schemas (HOs). (see Figure 3.1)

Dimensions are specific entities that individuals use to represent
events in the situation (e.g., size, shape, activities). These dimensions are
seen as learned and are either categorical or continuous. A particular category or point on a continuum was referred to as a position on a dimension.

Internal perceptions of relationships among positions on certain dimensions or awareness of recurring patterns of configurations among dimensions allow for the development of more abstract and general rules
regarding relationships among events. These abstract or general rules were
referred to as Lower Order Schemas (LOSs).

Through internal cognitive processes, individuals may recall and
cognitively manipulate selected dimensions of different LOSs, or entire
LOSs, and consequently develop more abstract and generalized schemas
based on relationships or configurations among dimensions and LOSs.
These are called Higher Order Schemas (HOSs). Several hierarchical levels
of HOSs might exist whereby each higher level is based upon conceptualized relationships and/or other configurations among lower level HOSs.
As Stotland and Canon (1972) claim, an HOS is a general and abstract
rule concerning regularities and relationships among events, reflected by
beliefs" about situations.

Stotland and Canon argue that this model is salient to PC because
individuals tend to use HOSs to interpret situations, although LOSs and
dimensions are involved. In short, the interpretation of environments "in
terms of their psychological meaning and significance is thought to be a
result of higher-order schemata, or beliefs about situations" (James &
Jones, 1976; James et al., 1978; James & Sells, 1981, p.277). For example, as James and Sells (1981) suggest, a cognitive association be-

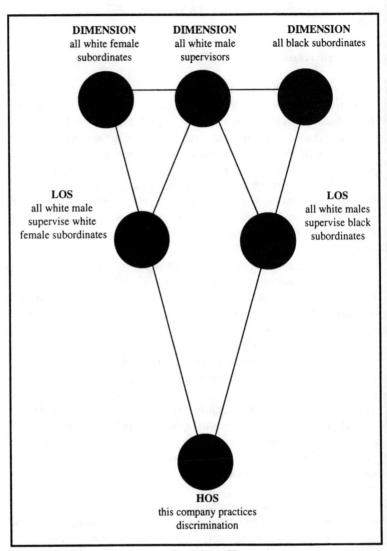

Figure 3.1: Perceptual Development: The Schema Theory

tween perceived nonrepetitiveness of tasks and experienced mental challenge may result in an HOS (belief) that the job is challenging.

HOSs of work environments are indicated by PC which involves perceptual/cognitive constructs. It can then be concluded that HOSs and PC reflect only abstract generalizations about situation and, thus, may not be tied directly to situational attributes and events (Stotland & Canon, 1972). James and Sells (1981) further suggest that "individuals have the capacity not only to process information and cognitive associations, but also cognitively to manipulate information and associations to create new knowledge" (p.277). In other words, situational events may be redefined to protect self-esteem or to preserve cognitive consistency with other beliefs.

The conclusions drawn from this theoretical paradigm agree that (a) PC measures are designed to represent HOSs as individuals report the end-point of the perceptual cognitive processes as reflected by beliefs about situations (HOSs) and (b) the HOSs included in PC measurements reflect the assumption that the individual is an active agent in constructing cognitive representations of situations/environments.

James and Jones (1976) proposed a "nomological net" model, a construct which refers to perceptions of salient aspects of organizational situations. This construct is similar to the proposed "cognitive schema" model. Nomological net theory provides a common denominator for theoretical developments of PC and HOSs. Conclusively, Psychological climate (PC) is a product of an intricate cognitive process which eventually gives meaning to a situation for an individual. Psychological climate measurements determine the end product of the cognitive process or the Higher-Order schema (HOS). But the concern that is pertinent to the objective of this study is the source of this cognitive process or Higher-Order Schemas (HOSs).

If indeed psychological climate (PC) is viewed as a set of HOSs (James et al., 1978) , then PC is the end result of the cognitive perceptual process. The consequent implication drawn from this conclusion is that to understand PC it is necessary to investigate and understand the individual in the person by situation (PXS) interaction. Field studies have suggested that climate perceptions are (a) significantly but weakly tied to situational measures (e.g., task context), (b) significantly related to position variables (e.g. hierarchical level), (c) significantly but weakly related to selected and nonaffective individual difference variable (e.g., intellectual aptitude), and (d) weakly and nonsignificantly related to PXS interactions. Research investigating the individual's culture and the way he/she perceives the organizational climate is absent. Of major importance is the suggestion that different individuals use different cognitive schemas (HOSs) to represent the same situations in the same environment as a result of, according to James et al. (1978), "differences in cognitive complexities, intelligence, social competencies, needs and so forth" (p. 793). The need to investigate the relationship between culture/ethnicity and PC has not been realized.

Summary of theories of perception development

In essence, the common thread that knits together all theories of perception is the cognitive structure phenomenon. The understanding of the sequencing of the steps in information processing has since the 1940s occupied the minds of many scholars, particularly those in the field of psychology.

Conclusively, the theories suggest that individuals "select" stimuli from the environment for a multiplicity of reasons. They then "organize" them in some identifiable pattern usually based on already encountered patterns in their environment and subsequently "interpret" the information again based on already established criteria inherited from their culture.

This perception process is of particular significance to the current investigation as it emphasizes the need for psychological climate theories to invest more effort in analyzing the individual as a psychological being. This study's review of the psychological climate theories found evidence of the influence of position in the organization, seniority, levels of pay and differences in leadership on variance in psychological climate perceptions (PC) among employees. The review has also realized an absence of investigations that establish the individual's culturally inspired cognition as the cause of any variance in PC perceptions among individuals in the organization. An understanding of the psychological being of the individual is critical to PC theory.

The Relationship Between Perception and Culture

Bowers (1973) and Argyle and Little (1972), as quoted by Ekehammer (1974), assert that "Individuals construe or perceive the same environment differently" (p.1034). Agreeing with this assertion, James et al. (1978) claim that the psychological environment may be different for different individuals. They further suggest that (a) individuals respond primarily to cognitive representations of the situation, (b) the cognitive representations can be described in terms that are psychologically meaningful, and (c) cognitive representations of the same situation may differ among individuals.

Samovar and Porter (1991), in *Communication Across Cultures,* claim that the last step in the perceptual process — interpretation and evaluation— is not the same in all people because this step is a learned process influenced primarily by culture. They state that "although sound waves impinge upon our eardrums and cause nerve impulses to be transmitted through our aural nerves in much the same way, how we interpret and evaluate what we hear is very much a function of our culture" (p.104). Culture is important to our perception of environments. Interpretations we make of events and situations in the environment are highly individualistic and represent a unique set of experiences in the culture in which we were raised.

Longstreet (1976) suggests that we are conditioned and moulded by our national, scholastic, and family ethnicity from the time of our birth to the age of twelve, the age at which we receive the capacity to intellectualize on our own. Between those early years, she says, the individual is most impressionable and is vulnerable to the internalizing of the stimuli around him/her. It is between these ages that we learn to cognize and to learn almost everything there is to know about behavior, value, meaning and so on. Even when the individual attains the potential to intellectualize, he/she has little capacity to choose or to change anything that has been already assigned to his/her ethnic behavior pattern.

We learn to interpret the world as we grow up interacting within our culture. By observing the way people around us behave, we learn how to interpret our world. Samover and Porter in *Communication Across Cultures* claim that it is "through this learning process, we not only develop the capacity to identify social objects and events, but to give those objects and events meaning and value" (p.104). The culture in which we are raised predominantly determines our beliefs, which are the basis for our values. Individuals' cognitive structure consists of many values that are organized into a value system which has been defined by Rokeach (1973) as " an enduring organization of beliefs concerning preferable modes of conduct or end-state existence along a continuum of relative importance" (p. 5). Values are linked to perception in that they are determinants of the interpretation and evaluation stage of the process. Culture also determines our view of the world, and each culture perceives a different reality. This occurs , according to Samovar and Porter in *Intercultural Communication (1991),* because people need to make observations and gather knowledge that makes sense within their particular cultural perspective. As the authors note, "how we view our universe, our position in it, what we value, how we think, and how we behave within that universe are all products of cultural learning" (p.116).

Triandis and Albert (1987) suggest that in the communication transaction across cultures the message which in essence represents the HOSs is subjected to a variety of manipulations as a result of cultural differences. The message, they argue, suffers from a lack of exact translation as well as loss of meaning when it is decoded in another culture. The source uses a particular cognitive framework which consists of "categories" or "dimensions" as labeled by Stotland and Canon (1972) and their "association" or "LOSs" organized into "schemata" or "HOSs" that have "affect" attached to them, " forming values, attitudes, expectations, norms, roles and reflecting unstated assumptions" (p.265). These, according to the authors, are the elements of subjective culture (norms, roles, belief systems, laws, values) which shape the encoding/decoding of the message or that they give meaning to the abstract. Samovar and Porter label them "sociocultural elements" which they also say have a direct and major influence on the meaning we develop for our perceptions. Also, Triandis (1980a) has established links between elements of subjective culture and social behavior. He writes, "An important aspect of culture is that it reflects shared meaning, norms, and values. Members of the same culture know 'the rules of the game' so that their interactions can be effective" (Triandis & Albert,1987, p.266).

Key dimensions that underlie the development of culture include perception, cognitive frames people carry with them, and patterns of action acceptable in various societies. Triandis and Albert (1987) suggest that cognitive frames are most important. These frames are the dimensions societies provide their members for processing information that has been perceived. Further, cognitive frames determine the emphasis that individuals from certain societies place on people, ideas, and action; on different values; on process versus goal, and on patterns of information process.

The cognitive frameworks used by the sender or encoder and receiver or decoder of the message are the sole determinant of the meaning that is attached to it. Meaning is a product of perception, so certainly the cognitive framework is the very same employed in the perception process or the information processing process. Culture, seems to be at the very core of cognitive processing, which gives meaning to situations through the perception schema as advanced by Stotland and Canon in 1972.

Studies in the field

Support for this notion is evident in one of the basic approaches to cross-cultural studies as identified by Jacobson et al. (1962). This approach is aimed at identifying and manipulating differential cultural characteristics that are assumed or demonstrated to have a relationship to attitude formation and change.

Two of the primary uses of national differences have been made in attitude studies. The first assigns relative weight to cultural factors as opposed to other processes in the formation and development of attitudes. Gillespie and Allport (1995) attributed differences in attitudes among countries to regional, national, or subcultural factors. They pursued this problem in a study of perceptual illusion. Measurements were taken among subjects from cultures assumed to be more or less likely to provide "relevant past experiences" with respect to perceptual phenomena. Differences in reported perception of the trapezoid window illusion were attributed to cultural influences and similarities to basic human psychophysiological processes.

The second specifies national differences that are used as a basis for the understanding of hypothesized or demonstrated relationships among patterns of attitudes or among attitudes and other factors. One such example is the simultaneous studies conducted by Jacobson and Schachter (1954) and the institute for Social Research in Oslo, Norway that examined the relationship between perceived threats of war and attitude towards international, domestic, and personal situations. In these studies, national differences were used as a basis for understanding the way in which so many of the relationships vary in size, direction and significance in different countries, the way they seem modified by specific national and international situational factors, by the historically-given structures of political forces, by the dominant policies, by majority-minority relations, by the ongoing communication processes in mass media and in the larger organizations. Interestingly, the conclusions in both approaches are that differences or variations in attitudes and perceptions were attributed to cultural influences.

In the academic years 1974-75, a series of perceptual exercises were given to undergraduate and graduate students in education in two urban universities. The conclusions of this project conducted by Chachere (1977) endorsed the relationship between ethnicity and perceptions. The exercises were part of a study module, Cultural and Social Awareness in Education," developed to assist in the development of an awareness and understanding of some of the cultural and social factors that influence students and teachers in inner-city schools.

The project undertook the challenge of testing the hypotheses (1) that perception is influenced by socialization variants and (2) that individuals' perceptions will be based on their total value system. The study modules were taught to two classes, one predominantly white, middle-class students and the other, black, mainly inner-city students. The educational background of the white students was derived from suburban and parochial schools. Few contacts were made by these students with inner-city people, neither in their early educational years nor college years. The white population sample consisted of all education majors. The comparison group was black students from a predominantly black university who were educated primarily in inner-city schools, segregated by poverty and race. Their families' average income level was classified as slightly above poverty level and few of their socialization activities involved students from suburban areas.

The exercises involved the showing of slides that depicted positive and negative aspects of inner-city living. The slides were arranged in five categories: economics, physical, education, population, and political. Each students was asked to select twenty-five slides that best represented his/her personal impression of the inner-city and then place them into the five categories. The division of positive and negative was not known to the students prior to selection. Results reveal that the mean scores of the profiles for the white, middle-class students were consistently negative for all categories. On the other hand, the mean scores for the black students were higher in a more positive direction in all categories. Marked differences between black and white scores were noted in the education and population categories .

According to Chachere (1977), the interpretation of these results suggest that inner-city people do not perceive their families, education, nor life style in a particularly negative way, or they will not admit to such a negative perception" (p.332). The other group was looking at the externals of the inner-city in all categories and was viewing these from a perceptual point of view influenced by social processes of relative affluence. Chachere also examined the implications for the educating of inner-city students who hold positive perceptions of their life and education by teachers who have negative perceptual frameworks toward the schools and the population. This study simultaneously endorses the relationship between ethnicity/culture and perception.

Summary of the relationship between perception and culture and implications for psychological climate

A relationship between psychological climate and ethnicity/culture emerges following the review of the theories that postulate a relationship between perception and culture. Psychological climate (PC) perceptions reflect the psychological significance and meaning of situations to the individual. James and Jones (1976) believe that perceptions of situations and events in the organization are in fact products of higher order cognitive information processing, where the individual employs higher order schemas (HOSs) to interpret situational information. They posit that perceptions are indeed HOSs which are relatively abstract and generalized beliefs about situations, and reflect the psychological significance and meaning of the situation to the individual. James et al. (1979) claim that an HOS for a particular situation/event reflect beliefs about that situation/event. It is this HOS, in their judgment, that provides the primary source for interpreting incoming information that resembles it as that situation/event.

HOSs are the end result of a cognitive perceptual process and as the theories of Verderber (1987), Triandis and Albert (1987), Samovar and Porter (1991) and Chachere et al. (1977) reveal, perception is culturally inspired. With reference to the generally used process —selection, organization, and interpretation— perception theories suggest that selection is stimulated by interest, expectation and limitation of senses, while organization and interpretation are influenced by culture. Samovar and Porter (1991) in *Communication Across Cultures* claim that they are "learned processes influenced primarily by culture" (p.104).

The current study is predicated on James and Jones' (1979) prediction that different types of individuals will be attentive to different aspects of their environment in formulating perceptions of situation/events. In their study of correlates of subordinates' perceptions of their psychological influence on supervisors' decisions, they hypothesized that the relationship between situational events and psychological influence will vary across subgroups formed on the person variable moderator. They defined PC as the individual's cognitive representation of relatively proximal situational conditions, expressed in terms that reflect psychologically meaningful interpretations of the situation. They decided that psychological influence fitted within the boundaries of the definition because it was a cognitive representation of proximal conditions (participation events), and reflects a psychologically meaningful interpretation of the situation (i.e., subordinates' perceived influence on decisions made by the supervisors). It was consequently recommended that measures of psychological influence reflect psychologically meaningful cognitive representations of the proximal situation.

One of the major results derived from this study was that theoretical assumptions underlying a PC approach to work environment perceptions were empirically verifiable. Support was provided for the assumptions that individuals have the capacities to construct subjective environments that reflect assimilation toward learned cognitive dispositions and differential attention to selected aspects of situations. The findings confirmed that (1) individuals' perceptions of the same situation are likely to differ, and (2) the reasons for these differences are psychologically important. Conclusively, culture's influence on perception implies that the psychological climate experienced by an individual is determined by his/her culturally inspired cognitive framework. This study consequently predicts that the perceptions of the same situation/event by ethnically/culturally different individuals in the same organization will differ and the reasons for these differences will indeed be psychologically important.

The Philosophical Congruence Between Symbolic Interaction and Psychological Climate Theories

The Symbolic Interaction paradigm allows for the viewing of meaning as a creation of interactions among individuals and among individuals and symbols. To embrace this paradigm is to endorse the notion that meaning is derived from social interactions among people. This study uses the theory of Symbolic Interactionism to increases the understanding of the dynamics that underlie the cognitive social learning and interactional psychology theories, the two theories that provide the foundation for psychological climate (PC) theory.

A look at cognitive social learning and interactional psychology theories from a symbolic interaction perspective

Current interactional and cognitive theories postulate that individuals perceive situations in terms of their personal meaning. Symbolic Interaction is based on three premises, according to Blumer (1969): (1) "Human beings act toward things on the basis of the meaning that the thing has for them"; (2) "the meaning of such things is derived from or arises out of the social interaction that one has with one's fellows"; (3) these meaning are handled in, and modified through, an interpretive process used by the person in dealing with the things he encounters" (p.2).

This study suggests that there is an apparent conceptual congruence between the symbolic interaction premise which suggests that an individual uses an interpretive process to handle and modify meaning and Stotland and Canon's (1972) schema theory which suggests that cognitive developmental process occurs at the highest level of the hierarchical model (HOS). It endorses James et al.'s (1978) claim that PC is a set of HOSs.

This study employs Verderber's (1987) theory that is in fact a synthesis of other theories of the perception process to further understand the dynamics of the schema theory (Stotland & Canon, 1972). Based on this theoretical foundation, the study theorizes that as the individual selects the object, event or activity, he/she employs a"dimension," a learned entity used to represent events in the environment. He/she subsequently develops abstract and generalized rules regarding the relationship among events "(LOS)" in the attempt to organize the information into some identifiable pattern (LOSs). The individual then interprets/evaluates the event/ situation or relationship(s) using his/her existing knowledge and the status of the current situation as a foundation for interpretation, (HOS). According to perception theorists, Stotland & Canon (1972), among others, the individual is predisposed to interpretations unique to his/her existing internal perceptions of relationships among positions on certain dimensions, or awareness of recurring patterns of configurations among dimensions . It is at this juncture that meaning is established (see Figure 3.2). As Blumer (1969) suggests, "these meanings are handled and modified through an interpretive process used by the person in dealing with the thing he encounter" (p.2).

This research further posits that the higher-order schema (HOS) is the product of this modification and interpreting process. As Stotland & Canon (1972) suggest, the individual, through internal cognitive processes, may recall and cognitively manipulate selected dimensions of different LOSs, or entire LOSs, thus developing more abstract and generalized schemas based on relationships or configurations among dimensions and LOSs. These abstractions and generalizations are referred to HOSs.

The current study postulates that there is a role for ethnicity/culture in the creation of meaning and inevitably in the perceptual process. Blumer's (1962) second premise that underlies the Symbolic Interaction theory suggests that meaning of situations or things is derived from or arises out of the social interaction that one has with one's fellows. This study endorses this premise but posits that this predisposition towards meaning as a result of interactions occurs very early in an individual's cultural life. The individual, prior to any encounter with other people,

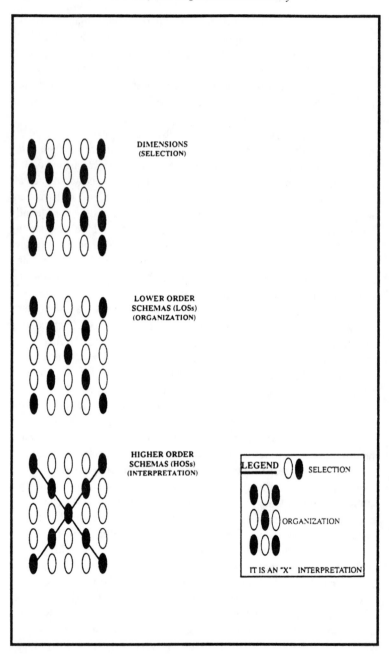

Figure 3.2: The Perceptual Development Process

with situations, or with events after age twelve (the age at which he/she is in complete command of his/her abstract intellectual powers) is already predisposed to a specific interpretation process. This interpretation process has been determined, according to Longstreet (1978), "primarily through the individual's early contacts with family, neighbors, friends, teachers, and others, as well as his/her immediate environment of the home and neighborhood" (p.19). This portion of cultural development, most of which occurs between birth and age twelve, Longstreet refers to as "ethnicity." The pertinence of this portion of the enculturation process has been neglected in the study of PC.

Also based on Triandis & Albert's (1987) theory of cultural development, this research posits that as the individual is socialized or interacts in his society/culture, he/she develops a particular cognitive framework which consists of 'categories' and their 'associations' organized into 'schemata' that have 'affect' attached to them, "forming values, needs, attitudes, expectations, norms, roles and reflecting unstated assumptions." According to these scholars, perceptions, cognitive frames people carry with them, and patterns of action acceptable in various societies are the key dimensions that underlie the development of culture.

Consequently, this study theorizes that cognitive frames are a product of the enculturation or socialization process that occurs early in an individual's life. It is these ethnically inspired cognitive frames that provide the individual with a structure for the processing of meaning and the development of perception as he/she interprets events or situations in the particular environment.

The levels of abstractions in the hierarchical schema model (dimensions, lower-order schemas (LOSs), and higher-order schemas (HOSs)) are salient to the study of psychological climate because, according to Stotland &Canon (1972), individuals tend to use HOSs to interpret situations (although LOSs and dimensions are involved). Individuals, however, do not introspect and report the perceptual-cognitive processing involved at arriving at HOSs; they report the conclusion of the perceptual-cognitive processing, as reflected by beliefs about situations. As a consequence, psychological climate (PC) has been deemed synonymous to higher-order schemas (HOSs) by James et al. (1978).

The study further realizes PC's subjection to conflict between HOSs openness to change and the tendency to preserve abstract, familiar, and valued beliefs about situations As James & Sells (1981) posit, HOSs are learned based on developmental experiences. Embracing cognitive processing as being a derivative of the enculturation process leads to the assumption that individuals with different learning experiences and synthesizing capabilities may employ different HOSs to interpret the same environmental attributes and events and consequently experience different PC perceptions and vice versa. It is important to note that once learned, HOSs are resistant to change because they are abstract, generalized and are familiar and valued by the individual. Jones & Gerard (1967) postulate that they are not influenced by inconsistencies between existing HOSs and specific situation events.

Stotland & Canon (1972), Jones & Gerard (1967), and Erdelyi (1974) note that HOSs and consequently PC perceptions are predisposed to constructing a subjective reality which evolves around products of cognitive frames such as existing (or desired) needs, values, and self-concepts. Consequently, individuals with different needs, self-concepts, and values which reflect different learning experiences will differ in their perception of the environment or PC perceptions (Bowers, 1973; Erdelyi, 1974; James et al. 1978,1979; Jones & Gerard, 1967). It can be concluded that HOSs or PC perceptions are a function of person variable and person- by- situation (PxS) interactions.

A corollary assumption made from this theoretical framework is that the PC experienced is a product of the individual's interpretation of the situation or event with which he/she interacts. The interpretation is a function of the cognitive schemas that his/her culture provides for understanding the situation/event. More specifically, it can be assumed that individuals of different ethnic/cultural backgrounds within an organization will interpret/ perceive the same organizational situation/event in different ways.

This study uses Longstreet's (1978) definition of "ethnicity" as that portion of cultural development that occurs before the age when an individual is in complete command of his/her abstract intellectual powers. She has distinguished between family, scholastic, and national ethnicity and suggests that these are three aspects of culture that determines the development of ethnicity. Consequently, an individual's ethnicity predisposes him/her to cognize or perceive things in ways that are unique to his/her culture.

Summary of the philosophical congruence between symbolic interaction and psychological climate theories

Philosophically speaking, the theory of Symbolic Interaction converges with the Cognitive Social Learning and Interactional Psychology theories. They all posit a relationship between enculturation and symbolic interaction with others within specific cultures. Meaning is created as the individual encounters and interacts with individuals and objects in his/her environment. It is through this process that the individual becomes enculturated; he/she attaches meanings to or interprets situations in accordance with how it has been learned through his/her interaction with others. According to Longstreet (1978), this enculturation process occurs early in life. After the age of twelve, she suggests, it is difficult to reconstruct any learning that has already taken place.

This research uses the Symbolic Interaction theory as the philosophical foundation theory from which this investigation operates. It detects the philosophical similarity between the theories used to understand the dynamics of the psychological climate (PC) theory and the Symbolic Interaction theory.

CHAPTER 4

The Cognitive and Ethnic Development of African-, European-, and Latin-Americans in the United States

This study recognizes that culture/ethnicity is the foundation for the development of cognitive structures. Anthropologists such as Donald Campbell, and Marshall Segal, among others, have extended the interest in ethnic differences in information processing back to the late 1940s and in the turn of the century. The results of those studies have been confirmed by recent scholars such as Samovar & Porter (1991) and Triandis & Albert (1987), among others.

Femminella (1979) refers to information processing as "any and all of the behavior engaged in by individuals as they deal with experience intellectually. That is, it includes learning, analyzing, expressing, or, stated from a cognitive learning perspective, ordering one's world" (p. 228). "Cognitive style" has been referred to as the characteristic way in which an individual conceptually organizes his/her environment. The common thread that holds all theories on cognitive style together is the emphasis on the structure rather the content of thought. Structure refers to the way in which the cognition is organized. One well-known example is that of

Witkins' black and white optical illusion that can be perceived either as two white profiles or a black vase. Those who perceive it to be faces are considered to be "field-dependent," individuals who are more dependent on the ground highlighting the figure, thus focusing on relationships between the figure and the ground. On the other hand, the "field independent" person sees the vase because they are not confused by the ground. Such individuals are characterized as perceiving analytically, easily extracting figures from irrelevant contexts.

Much has been done on the cognitive style phenomenon. Berry (1976) has developed a model of "differentiation" which he promotes as the ideal model for the study of cross cultural research on cognitive styles. Scholars employed "cognitive mapping," a process of testing and developing profiles on individual students' epistemological styles in an attempt to apply cognitive theory to individuals. Preliminary results of some studies seem to indicate , claims Femminella, that differential cognitive styles exist between African Americans, Puerto Ricans, and non-differentiated white groups.

These results have implications for the philosophical foundation of this study which examines the psychological climate experienced by African American, Euro-American, and Latin American students. Psychological climate is the product of the perception (cognitive structuring of information) of the climate of the college in which these students are educated and live. Also, central to the success of this study is an understanding of the ethnic backgrounds, family heritages, and evolving social class and life-styles of African Americans Euro-Americans, and Latin Americans in the United States.

This chapter consequently analyzes the ethnic differences between the three ethnic groups in the United States. It begins by analyzing the historical background of the ethnic groups in the United States. It further examines the evolution of the family and the scholastic and national heritages of each of the groups in an attempt to understand their cognitive developments and the differences between them.

Ethnic Backgrounds of Latin Americans, Euro-Americans and African Americans in the United States

An in-depth historical or anthropological analysis of the cultures of African Americans, Euro-Americans, and Latin-Americans will certainly increase the understanding of the ethnic differences that characterize and determine their cognitions and perceptions. However, the very nature of this research has provided boundaries for a review of literature that does not include an in-depth anthropological analysis.

This review provides a brief look at the family, scholastic, and national ethnicities (Longstreet, 1978) of the three subcultural groups through the analysis of pertinent subgroup characteristics with an emphasis on the family structure and backgrounds. This emphasis is inspired by the belief that the strength of the family is the determinant of the extent of influence of any potential national and scholastic ethnicity. In other words, what is learned in the family, especially during pre-school years, provides a foundation around which other influences revolve. This review emphasizes not only the salient characteristics of the family heritages of the three ethnic groups but also the similarities and differences among them.

Latin Americans in the United States

The over fifteen million Latin Americans in the US are indeed a heterogeneous population consisting mainly of Mexican and Spanish settlers from Mexico, Puerto Rico, Cuba and other Spanish-speaking countries. Some of the differences between these subgroups are great. Moore and Pachon (1985) claim that each subgroup "became part of the larger American population in a different manner. Each faced difference experiences in the larger American population in a different manner. Each lived through different economic, political, and environmental situations" (p. 1). Each group has a different sense of its own identity.

Despite differences in political, economic, social and at times environmental situations of their countries of origin, these groups are treated as one group in the US. Because of the growth and acceptance of the idea, "Hispanics" have become a national minority. One reason for this convergence is that all segments of the Hispanic community are predominantly urban and many are locked into poverty and face prejudices and discrimination.

Another reason for this unification is that the Hispanic populations are increasingly being treated by the larger society as a group with common practices and problems. Thus, they too have found it necessary to unite to battle the injustices that confront them as a group. Another salient reason is that subpopulations are beginning to disperse outside of the traditional areas, and accompanying this dispersal is a very large increase in their total numbers. It is consequently reasonable to think of all segments of the American Spanish speaking population as "Hispanics."

The Latin American family heritage

The US Census reliably indicates the "deep poverty" of American Hispanics. They have predicted that this poverty will dominate the lives of many Hispanics for years to come. The US Bureau of the Census (1972-1982) reveals that almost a quarter of Mexican-American families and almost a third of all Puerto Ricans families were living in poverty. The poverty is increasing. The percentages increased from 26 percent in 1981 to almost 30 percent in 1983. In the same year 53 percent of Mexican-American and Puerto Rican families headed by women were poor; this is identical to the percentage of Blacks and in all instances double that of white female-headed households. Poor housing is a direct consequence of this poverty.

Latin Americans place significant value on families, communities and churches. It is these institutions that protect their culture from the erosions of assimilation. Their social structures and culture were persistent enough to demand new theories such as the ones put forward by Moore and Pachon (1985) who postulate that Latin Americans stand in "symbolic opposition to the dehumanization and depersonalizing demands of the dominant society. Thus family, community, language, and culture are a source of pride for many Hispanics. Often they are contrasted to an Anglo culture and an Anglo family structure that is seen as cold, shallow, and uncaring" (p. 88).

However, as many young Hispanics move closer to the dominant society, as urbanization increases, and as new migrants continue to come in, Hispanic institutions consequently change. Even though there may be slight diversity in thinking among this group, cultural values remain salient. First-generation people are immigrants from the homeland; the second-generation referring to their children and subsequent generations, is expected to be more acculturated to the dominant society. For the Hispanics, however, assimilation is minimized because they are one of the few ethnic groups in the US that are still immigrating in large numbers. Consequently, "the relationship of Hispanics to their community is far more complex in terms of legal status, age, and class than most other ethnic groups.... There are Hispanics who are living in the United States long before Anglos, are tenth-generation Americans, and are still largely unacculturated" (Moore & Pachon, 1985, p. 90). The Puerto Ricans, especially, move back and forth to their country, tend to retain strong ties to their homeland, and do not adapt to the US because they have no stake in the country.

The preeminence of the family remains particularly strong in Latin American culture. The Latin American has a deep consciousness of his membership in a family as he thinks of his importance as being tied to his family membership. It is a characteristic that is an elemental thing among the poor as opposed to the wealthy. The world to the Latin American consists of " a pattern of intimate personal relationships, and the basic relationships are those of his family. His confidence, his sense of security and identity, are perceived in his relationship with others who are his family" (Fitzpatrick, 1976, p. 195).

The Latin American family is an extended one and the superiority of the man in not to be undermined. Moore and Pachon (1985) say that "'Machismo' is a particular cultural definition of masculinity" (p.96). Fitzpatrick (1976) supports this fact by observing that "the man expects to exercise the authority in the family; he feels free to make decisions without consulting his wife; he expects to be obeyed when he gives commands" (p. 197). As the middle class grows, this role is very slowly being redefined, but in contrast to the values of the dominant American society, the Hispanic woman occupies a subordinate role. Bonilla (1964) concluded in his study of a rural Puerto Rican community that migration had destroyed the patriarchal structure, causing women and young people to move away from the traditional roles.

Conclusively, this study realizes that as the Hispanics move into an institution dominated by any other ethnic group they bring with them a culture almost untouched by an assimilation process. The strength of the family structure has served to instill in them a cognitive structure that provides them with a set of beliefs and values that are unique to the Hispanic culture. Consequently, as Hispanic students exist within the university environment, the strength of their culture prevails and provides them with a cognitive framework from which they perceive the environment.

What distinguishes the Latin American from the Euro-American?

This study has found fundamental differences in cultural values between Euro-Americans and Latin-Americans. It calls on the works of Diaz-Guerrero (1967) which concentrates on the contrasts between US and Mexican cultures. He found that:

The historical traditional pattern of the United States will produce individuals who are active .... They will be independent, individualistic, autonomous, oriented toward achievement, competitive, somewhat impulsive and aggressive, and rather tense and nervous. The Mexican historical-socio-cultural pattern, on the other hand, will produce individuals who are obedient, affiliative, interdependent, orderly, cooperative, not oriented toward achievement, and not self-initiated. (p.125)

Diaz-Guerrero also concludes that when a member of the US culture experiences stress, the solution is usually to modify the environment, whether physical, interpersonal, or social. The Mexican resolves the same problem by modifying himself to with the environment (p. xviii). Of major importance to this study is Diaz-Guerrero's conclusion that Euro-Americans tend to be more complex and differentiated in cognitive style to the Mexican.

Moore and Pachol (1985) contend that differences in cognitive styles refer to particular ways of perceiving, organizing, being influenced by , and acting on reality. "In effect," they say, "children are taught how to learn by their cultures" (p.126). They have restated Holtzman's position as he distinguishes between "field dependent" learning, which is more characteristic of "nurturant, affiliative, socially sensitive, initiative individuals" and "field independent" learning which is characterized by analytical and scientific individuals. According to them, research has confirmed that Hispanics in America are much more "field dependent" than Euro-Americans. This finding is critical to the research objectives of the current study.

The African American Family Heritage

In 1960, Shannon and Shannon conducted a study of Chicano, black, and Anglo migrants to Racine, Wisconsin, to determine the relationship between the tenacity of traditional values and the income of the individual. Interestingly, they found that Mexican-Americans and black migrants into this city have a very similar world view, one that is dramatically different from the world view of the Anglo Americans even when the income was controlled. They concluded that the minority experience may be as much of a determinant of values as is the particular cultural heritages.

Like the Latin American, the African American, has a strong sense of family, a value that evolved from the rigors of slavery. Staples (1976) claims that "it was in the family that the slave received affection, companionship, love, and empathy with his sufferings under this peculiar institution. Through his family, he learned how to avoid punishment, to cooperate with his fellow slaves and to retain some semblance of his self esteem" (p. 224). Another important function of the slave family was to socialize the child, to cushion him from the shock of bondage, to teach him values that were different from those of the masters so as to provide him with a frame of reference for his self esteem besides the master's.

Another factor that must be considered is that the number of black female-headed households is significantly larger than white female-headed households. This black phenomenon, according to Staples, is a direct result of socioeconomic forces. As the level of income rises in the black communities, so does the number of male-headed households. Very much like their Latin American counterparts, African Americans have a kinship network which is more extensive and cohesive than kinship bonds among the white population. United States census data reveals that a larger portion of blacks take relatives and extended families into their homes. Adams (1970) suggests that the strong kinship bonds can be attributed to the minority status of this group which stimulates the need for mutual aid and survival in a hostile environment. Whatever the reason, the extended family is very characteristic of the black kinship patterns similar to those found in African societies.

Matthews (1972) proposes that the African American needs to function as a corporate group because his identity is usually the group's identity and is always related to the remainder of the total black community. This author suggests that for African Americans, the black extended family is the functional unit of black community. Nobles (1972) concludes that the black family has always socialized its members to see no distinction between his personal self and other members of the family. Yet another product of this kinship is the inclusion of nonblood relatives who are referred to and treated like kinsmen, an example being the "brother" and "sister" relationship among black men and women who are unrelated by blood. This pattern of kinship is somewhat duplicated in the Latin American community but is absent in the Euro-American family structure.

Theories of the black matriarchy have been under tremendous scrutiny by scholars such as Ladner (1971) and many others who posit that an equalitarian pattern characterizes most black families. According to Ladner, while the black woman is strong and needed to be so in order for her family to survive, she was not necessarily dominant. She certainly, unlike her Anglo counterparts, had to work outside the home to supplement the income of her husband; therefore, she would have some input into any decision-making process in the household.

Evolving social class and life-styles of African Americans

The opportunities for blacks in education increased throughout the decades. With this improvement came a massive amount of mobility occurring in the black class structure. Beginning in the 1970s, a negligible number of blacks moved into the upper-class, about 30 percent moved into the middle-class, and the rest fell into the working class stratum, according to the US Bureau of Census.

Social class, for research purposes, has been defined as more than a person's income and educational level. Bernard (1966) has distinguished between the "acculturated" black family, those that have internalized Western norms , and the "externally adapted" black family, those that have adopted these norms superficially. He suggests that most middle-class black families have externally adopted these middle-class norms in order to obtain a "decent life."

Research has realized a significantly low family size of blacks in the middle-class as compared to blacks in the working class blacks. Ladner and Staples suggest that this is a result of blacks' realization of the direct link between low family income and large families. Despite the increasing numbers of blacks entering the middle class, they still work harder for fewer rewards. At the same level of education and occupation, black wages are still lower than whites. According to Hess, Markson and Stein (1988), "a typical white male high-school dropout earns more than a college educated black male, largely because of discrimination and the differing employment opportunities for the two races" (p.91).

With the increase of the diffusion of blacks into predominantly white suburbs, interracial relationships, racially integrated school systems, and increased television viewing has come the exposure to the majority cultural norms. This results in an opportunity for black acculturation and assimilation. The extent of assimilation can be measured from relatively high to absent. On one hand, there are those blacks who attempt to disregard anything that ties them to their race. Those born in this type of environment will consequently inherit an ethnicity that quite resembles that of the majority culture. On the other hand, there are those blacks who despite their everyday existence in the majority culture and demand separate facilities and organizations. Such is the case of black university students who form black student organizations and unions on predominantly white campuses. Also, there are those blacks who move into the suburbs but continue their social lives in the inner cities. Although the extended family may not exist together in the same household, there are those blacks who still provide emotional support and assistance to each other and other members of the black community. Staples (1976) points out that these are some of the actions that African Americans take to prevent racial integration from diluting their cultural unity.

Conclusively, this study realizes that there are similarities in the role of the family of Latin Americans and African Americans. The family institution has been a force in the lives of these two groups; it serves to buffer the forces of discrimination and prejudice meted out from the dominant culture. Changing societal circumstances have resulted in the evolution of thinking and behaviors among generations within these groups. They have, in some cases, eroded traditional values and philosophies as current generational members become acculturated in school systems that expose them to the majority cultural patterns. However, some basic values and worlds views that characterize each ethnic group perpetuate. The current study suggests that the extent of acculturation of the current generation of Latin American and African American is related to the strength of each family's cultural identity which has provided his/her ethnicity.

The Role of Scholastic Ethnicity in the Culture of the Latin American, African American and Euro-American

Longstreet (1978) posits that "there are roles that are ethnically learned, i.e., absorbed prior to the period between the ages ten and twelve such as those between daughter and father, and there are roles rationally and consciously assumed in one's adulthood such as those of a G. M. worker and a union organizer." (p.21). She suggests that the control we have over our actions in different roles depends to a large extent on the time in our lives that we assumed the roles.

Longstreet suggests that our roles as students have critical influences on our ethnic development. Many individuals enter school at the ages of five or six, some even earlier. They encounter all the bureaucratic traditions of the school culture and their by-products; these include modes of communication, modes of rewards and punishments, acceptable relationships between student and teacher, and student and student, and so on. This culture conditions the individual long before any existence of logic so that it contributes to his ethnicity. Again, this study accepts the importance of scholastic ethnicity on the individual's cultural formation, but suggests that this influence exists within the framework of the influencing family heritage.

Euro-American, Latin-Americans, and African-Americans born in the United States have all been through a school system which is constitutionally governed by a specific set of rules. Scholastic ethnicity, according to Longstreet, is likely to be a national phenomenon because the bureaucracy and the traditions of the public schools are very similar throughout the nation as well as across generations. Gradings, educational artifacts, periods, course offerings, and in most cases course contents have remained unchanged throughout several generations across the nation.

However, in more recent times, scholastic ethnicity has impacted the ethnicities to a greater extent as they have been influenced by circumstances such as mobility, mastermind computers, and paranoia of environmental pollution, among other things. Of critical concern to some scholars is the effect of these factors on the ethnicity of children whose family heritage in no way resembles that of the evolving scholastic ethnicity.

The primary source of the education of Latin-Americans and African-Americans is the public school, although the numbers entering the private and parochial schools are increasing. Private and parochial schools are attended by Euro-Americans. Public perceptions about and attitudes towards public schools have been negative. The difference in the cultures of the public and private schools has always been distinct. It is sometimes believed that public schools are characterized by inferiority of education (curriculum and standards), lack of discipline, use of drugs, lack of proper financial support, and low morale and self-esteem of the student body. However, some members of these groups have used the public school to their advantage and they are currently narrowing the gap between minorities and whites who enter college from high school. It is believed that the problems that are allegedly plaguing the public schools are indeed school problems in general in the United States. Longstreet's research concludes that the factors that underlie the problems of the public school are poverty, racial discrimination, social inequalities and lack of financial support. Also, the public school system that does not ensure effective teaching qualities. This study, however, has recognized that the underlying foundation of the problems is indeed the existence of an educational system, a system of scholastic ethnicity that is incompatible with the family ethnicity of the minority student. According to Femminella (1979):

It is important to note that the best style, the style that we believe everyone should use in learning, is determined by our value system. .... The tragedy in our society is that we do in fact prefer some of these styles over others, and we impose rewards and sanctions on them. Although different cognitive styles probably existed between European ethnic groups (and among minority groups), it is only as a result of integrated education that we are beginning to recognize these differences and the specific values inherent in each of the different styles. (p.115)

However, according to Longstreet (1978), because the individual adopts the role of student at such an early age, that role influences his/her ethnic development. There will consequently be implications for those students whose family ethnicity diverge extensively from the ethnicity of the scholastic system. The implication of critical concern to this study is that of the student whose perceptions were influenced by a scholastic ethnicity other than that of the United States.

The National Ethnicity

Is there a general American ethnicity, a set of ethnically learned behaviors that are shared by most Americans despite their specific family heritages? Longstreet (1978) suggests that the scholastic ethnicity can be considered part of the national ethnicity. She postulates that there are traits that are unique to the American experience, traits such as hamburger stands, miles of highways, millions of cars, appliances, football, and specific types of television programming, to mention a few. These traits are characteristically American as they become part of the whole American experience. She continues, "These nationally experienced phenomena usually filter through to young children via the adults with whom they are in direct contact, normally members of their family" (p.24).

Despite differences in family heritages, everyone shares in this American culture and consequently reacts to the same phenomena. Longstreet postulates that television is a salient national phenomenon that has significant impact on the average pre-schooler whatever his/her family heritage. She further suggests that individuals from different ethnic groups in the US are culturally closer than individuals of their ethnic groups from different countries/cultures.

Another point of critical concern to scholars who study the dynamics of the minority existence in America is the incompatibility of minority family heritage with the general national ethnicity. W. E. B. DuBois examines the "duality that plagues the black world as he talks about "one ever feels his twoness...an American, a negro, two souls, two thoughts, two unreconciled strivings..." (p.17). In like manner, the African American, Latin American and Euro-American born in the US will all experience the general national ethnicity. However, the current study posits that the family ethnicity acts as a mediator between the individual and the scholastic and national ethnicities.

This research by no means confuses socioeconomic or social class backgrounds with ethnicity. It has simply provided some insight into the backgrounds of the different ethnic groups to ensure an understanding of the differences that characterize their existences. Each ethnic group shares a system of beliefs and practices that is unique to the others. For example, with regard to infancy, Coll (1990) posits that such scholars as Rebelsky, Super, and Zeskind believe that cultures differ in their views of the fragility of the newborn, their perceptions and responses to crying, and the value of encouraging certain developmental skills. Consequently, we can see that infants of different ethnic groups are exposed to care-giving environments that are different in cultural beliefs and care-giving practices. According to Ogbu (1981) and Levine (1977) , adults inculcate through different techniques and different cognitive, linguistic, motivational and social competencies; these competencies are considered relevant to their cultural milieu.

Of utmost significance to this study is the family heritage. To understand the historical evolution of the family heritage of the different ethnic groups is to understand the foundation of practices, beliefs, and values that characterize the groups. Children at the age of ten or twelve who were born in the United States are bearers of their family's ethnic heritage, an American ethnic heritage, and a scholastic heritage. However, because of the significance of the family heritage, they will differ in the way that they perceive and react to the world.

This study suggests that individuals who share the same family heritage will share similar cognitions and perceptions of the environment. Those who share the same family heritage but different scholastic and national ethnicities will not share significantly similar cognitions and perceptions of the environment. Those individuals that share different family heritages but similar scholastic and national ethnicities will not cognize or perceive their environments similarly. The strength of the family heritage determines the extent of influence of the scholastic and national ethnicities.

Summary of Ethnic Differences among Latin-Americans, African-Americans and Euro-Americans

This review of the literature that speaks to ethnic differences among the groups reveals commonalities of experiences between the Latin American and African American. The salience of the family, the backlashes of the injustices of discrimination, the experience of prevalent poverty are attributions of the dynamics that underlie the lives of African Americans and Latin-Americans in the United States historically as well as currently. The majority of Euro-Americans, on the other hand, have evolved from an historic experience of poverty and its by-products to lives that are by US Census Bureau standards considered middle and upper class.

This review reveals an influence of not only family heritage on the early life of the individual but also the influence of what Longstreet (1978) calls scholastic and national ethnicity. Family, national, and scholastic ethnicity combine to enculturate the individual and provide him/her with an ethnicity that serves him/her throughout life.

Studies that investigate ethnic differences with relation to cognitive structures date back as far as the 1940s. The concept of cognitive structure has occupied the minds of many scholars as revealed by this literature review. Ogbu and Levin have concentrated some of their efforts on the differences in child rearing among different ethnic groups in the United States. Basco and his associate invested some efforts in determining the differences in learning styles among different ethnic groups in the US, and Berry developed a model of "differentiation" which he promotes as an ideal model with which to study ethnic differences in cognitive styles.

Results of these numerous studies fundamentally endorse the ethnic differences in cognitive structure hypothesis, which is critical to the foundation of the psychological climate theory. The present investigation focuses on that very foundation of cognitive structural differences among ethnic groups. In its review of psychological climate theories and studies, it found no investigations of hypotheses that suggest an influence of the individual's culture in the determination of the psychological climate that he/she experiences. The results of the current study provides the field of psychological climate with perception data that can serve as fertile ground for the study of the development of psychological climate perceptions.

PART TWO

CHAPTER 5

Investigation into the Relationship Between Ethnicity and Psychological Climate Perception

As the literature review in part 1 reveals, African-Americans and Latin Americans in the United States share similar experiences of racial discrimination, pervasive poverty, evolving social classes and strong family influences. Using Longtreet's theory on ethnicity which suggests that individuals who share similar national, scholastic, and family experiences will tend to share similar ethnicities, this research attempts to determine if university students' psychological climate perceptions of diversity in their institution is indeed influenced by their ethnicity. This chapter describes the data collection and analysis procedures used in this study. It discusses in detail the research setting as well as the research procedures which include sample selection, sample description and instrumentation. It describes the statistical analysis used and presents the results that answer the research questions. The results are presented in the following sequence: (1) reliability and frequency scores for scales, (2) PC perception among African-American, Euro- American and Latin American student samples, (3) PC perception differences within (a) African-American students, (b) Euro-American students, and (c) Latin American student samples, and (4) relationship between students' ethnicity, psychological climate perceptions and their satisfaction with the university.

Research Setting

This study was conducted on a private, non-sectarian, four-year university located on a 340-acre suburban campus in the United States. It enrolls approximately 3,500 undergraduate and 1,200 graduate students. The current study surveyed 250 of the undergraduate students from across all disciplines and classifications.

The college enrolls predominantly Euro-American students who make up approximately 80% of the student body. Some 6% of the students are African-Americans, 4% are Latin Americans and the remaining 10% constitute Asian or Pacific Islanders as well as American Indian or Alaskan natives and students whose race or ethnicity is unknown. At the time this study was conducted, the college enrolled 2,340 white students, 139 African-American students, and 109 Latin American students in its undergraduate programs. This study's sample was drawn from this population.

Research Questions

This research responds to the following questions:

1. Do psychological climate (PC) perceptions vary among African-American, Latin American, and Euro-American students?

2. Do psychological climate (PC) perception vary among (a) African-American students, (b) Euro-American students, and (c) Latin American students with regard to (i) type of high school they attended, (ii) the location of the high school they attended, (iii) their country of birth, (iv) the country of their parents' birth, and (v) their gender?

3. Is there a relationship between student's ethnicity, their psychological climate (PC) perceptions and concomitant satisfaction with the university?

Procedure: Survey method

The sensitive nature of this study demanded a guaranteed anonymity of the respondents so that sensitive questions can be answered candidly. Consequently, the self-report questionnaire was chosen as the means of data collection for this descriptive survey study. The self-report questionnaires eliminate the biases in responses that tend to occur in face-to-face interviews.

This research employed both the mail questionnaire and group administration of questionnaire methods. The mail questionnaire method was used only to ensure an adequate response rate from two of the three ethnic groups being surveyed. African-American and Hispanic Americans make up only 10% of this college's undergraduate population and are not concentrated in any one discipline; this made the administration of questionnaires to groups of these students almost impossible. However, questionnaires were group administered to White American students who make up a significant percentage of students in classes at this college.

Wimmer and Dominick (1983) have discovered that group administration of questionnaires "combines features of the mail survey and the personal interview" (p. 129). These scholars further find that the group administered survey occurs when a group of respondents are gathered in the same location and are given a copy of a questionnaire and are asked to respond to the questions individually and at their own pace. The respondents are allowed to ask questions when it is necessary. Group administration of a questionnaire, like the personal interview, allows for the establishment of a degree of subject-researcher rapport, which aids in the successful completion of the task. This method also ensures a high response rate since completed questionnaires are collected before respondents leave the room. The opportunity for researchers to answer questions or handle problems that might arise generally means that fewer items are left blank or answered incorrectly. On the negative side, Wimmer and Dominick (1983) suggest that group administration of questionnaires makes it possible for respondents to interact and compare answers; this has the potential for making the situation difficult for the researcher to control.

Separating the environments in which ethnically different respondents completed questionnaires became a necessity created by the inability to include an adequate sample of two of the three ethnic groups (Latin Americans and African-Americans) in the group administration process. This inadvertently became an advantage in light of the fact that portions of the survey may have been perceived as sensitive by students of the different ethnic groups. According to Wimmer and Dominick (1983), the fact is that some studies may not use samples that should be tested together in agroup. "They state that surveys often require responses from a wide variety of people, and mixing respondents together may bias theresults" (p. 130).

According to Waliezer & Weiner (1978), the single most trouble-some aspect of mailing questionnaires is the problem of nonresponse. Scientists have invested a lot of time on the development of strategies to avoid this problem. Linsky's (1975) review of literature in the area shows some factors that are used to increase response rates. They are (1) follow-ups, (2) pre-contact of respondents, (3) "high powered" postage such as special deliveries, (4) prepaid cash rewards, and (5) sponsorship by an important agency/institution/person.

However, there are advantages to the mail surveys, according to Wimmer and Dominick (1983). These surveys are the only way to gather information from people who live in hard-to-reach places, or in the case of this study, people who are hard to reach. They also help with selective sampling through the use of specialized mailing lists. Yet another advantage of this method is that it provides anonymity. Questionnaires can be completed in the privacy of the respondent's own home or dorm room, as in the case of this study, so that sensitive questions are more likely to be answered candidly. Mail surveys also eliminate researcher's bias since there is no contact between researcher and respondent.

Sample Selection

This study sampled 250 students. Three ethnic groups of students from across all majors and classifications were sampled by means of the nonprobability sampling method of purposive sampling. Purposive or "judgment" sampling is building a sample which reflects the characteristics and properties that are critical to the population under investigation. In this study, the selection of all sample groups was based on the nonprobability method of purposive sampling. Questionnaires were group administered to 98 white undergraduates across disciplines and classifications during four sessions of Speech Communication classes by means of purposive sampling. This course was considered ideal since it comprised predominantly white American undergraduate students from all disciplines, classifications, and ages. Ninety-six percent of the students were Euro American and 5% were African-American and Latin American. Surveys were retrieved from African-American and Latin American students through the mail and by personal collection methods.

This survey collection method produced 151 completed questionnaires from the African-American and Hispanic population. Ninety-eight were African-American respondents and 53 were Hispanic American.

Description of Sample

The sample of students who participated in this study consisted of 98 African-Americans, 53 Hispanic Americans and 98 white Americans a total of 249 students. The actual number of surveys collected was 256, four of which were Asian American and three could not be included in the survey because of inadequate biographical information.

Data were collected from 143 females and 106 males across ethnic groups, majors and classifications. Students ranged in ages from 18 to 50 with the majority, 165, being between ages 19 and 21. Respondents were undergraduates across all majors. Eighty-three freshmen, 49 sophomores, 59 juniors and 56 seniors identified their classification in the survey; two did not.

Two hundred and seven of the 249 survey respondents were born in the US, while the remaining 42 immigrated to the US between the ages of 2 months and 21 years. Approximately 70% of students surveyed have parents who were born in the US.

The majority of respondents' parents have completed high school. Forty-nine percent of the students responding were raised in suburban areas, 12% in a rural area, 15.7% in an urban area, 10% in a small city, and 12% in a large city. Of all respondents, 67.5% attended public school and 54.2% of them attended schools located in the suburbs; thirty-five percent attended schools in an urban area and 9.6% in a rural area.

Forty-five of the 249 respondents surveyed reported a family gross combined income of $75,000 and above while 40 reported a combined family gross income of $20,000 and below. The remaining 164 fell evenly between $20,000 and $75,000.

Tables 5.1 and 5.2 presents a description of the analysis sample for students classified by crossing ethnicity with gender, area in which student was raised, type and location of high school attended and income. The table reflects that:

1. The sample size of the African-American female (63) was disproportionately larger than that of the African-American male (35) as compared with the male-female sample of the other two groups whose samples were 29 to 23 and 50 to 48 for the Hispanic and African-American samples respectively.

2. The majority of African Americans (43.8%) were raised in a suburban area. The majority of White Americans (53.3%) were also raised in the suburbs while Hispanic Americans

(28.3%) were raised in suburban and 26.4% were raised in an urban area.

3.   The majority of African Americans (82%) and White Americans (69.4%) attended public high schools, with the majority of Hispanic Americans (43.4%) attending a private high school; only 35.8% of them attended public high schools.

4.   The majority of White Americans attended high schools in a suburban area (75.5%). The majority of African Americans attended high schools in an urban area (49.5%) with 41.1% attending school in a suburban area. The majority of Hispanic American students (50.9%) attended high schools in an urban area while 41.5% of Hispanics attended a high school that was located in the suburbs.

5.   Seventy-one percent of White American students; 20% of Hispanic American and 8% of African American students came from families whose gross annual income was $75,000 and above. Forty -seven and one half percent of African American students' combined gross family income was $25,000 and under. Thirty-seven and one half percent of Hispanic American students and 15% of White American students came from families with a combined gross family income of $25,000 and under.

Instrumentation

The 14-page questionnaire comprised seven parts of 159 items representing 24 scales constructing 9 dimensions. Part 1 included 12 biographical questions. Part 11 measured the psychological climate (PC) perceptions that students hold of the college. The third part measured students' perception of social interaction among pairs of ethnically different students on the campus. The fourth part measured students' perception of the success of the student groups on the campus. In the fifth part of the survey, students were asked their personal inter-ethnic relations. Part V1 measured the level of pride that students had in the college and the seventh section questioned their general satisfaction with the college.

Part 1 asked for biographical data: (i) age, (ii) gender, (iii) classification, (iv) major, (v) ethnic group, (vi) country of birth, (vii) age at which

ETHNICITY	GENDER		AREA RAISED					TYPE OF HIGH SCHOOL			HIGH SCHOOL LOCATION		
	Female	Male	Rural	Sub-Urban	Urban	Small City	Large City	Parochial	Private	Public	Rural	Sub-urban	Urban
African American	64.2%	35.7%	9.4%	43.8%	17.7%	11.5%	17.7%	9.2%	8.2%	82.7%	9.5%	41.1%	49.5%
Hispanic-American	55.7%	44.2%	7.5%	28.3%	26.4%	15.1%	22.6%	20.8%	43.4%	35.8%	7.5%	41.5%	50.9%
White American	51.0%	48.9%	17.5%	67.0%	8.2%	6.2%	1.0%	15.3%	15.3%	69.4%	11.2%	75.5%	13.3%
Total Percentage (Mean)	56.9%	42.9%	11.4%	46.3%	17.4%	10.9%	13.7%	15.1%	22.3%	62.6%	9.4%	52.7%	37.9%

Table 5.1
Percentage distribution of subgroups of student sample.

ETHNICITY	FAMILY GROSS INCOME						
	$20,000 and Under	$21,000 to $30,000	$31,000 to $00,000	$41,000 to $50,000	$51,000 to $60,000	$61,000 to $70,000	$71,000 and Above
African-American	64.2%	35.7%	9.4%	43.8%	17.7%	11.5%	17.7%
Hispanic-American	55.7%	44.2%	7.5%	28.3%	26.4%	15.1%	22.6%
White American	51.0%	48.9%	17.5%	67.0%	8.2%	6.2%	1.0%
Total Percentage (Mean)	56.9%	42.9%	11.4%	46.3%	17.4%	10.9%	13.7%

Table 5.2: Percentage Distribution of Subgroups of Student Sample (Family Combined Gross Income).

immigrated to the US, (viii) country of parents' birth, (ix) parents' level of education, (x) area in which raised, (xi) type and location of high school, and (xii) family gross combined income.

The second part of the survey instrument, the psychological climate (PC) aspect, accounts for 20 PC scales measured by 101 items. This part of the instrument uses the PC survey instrument that was developed by the Institute of Behavioral Research; Texas Christian University, Forth Worth, Texas in 1980 and was employed in a study they conducted en- titled "Identification of Perceived Environmental Factors Associated with Student Adjustment, Laboratory Performance, and Satisfaction in the Air Traffic Control Specialist Training Program." The study focused on "stu- dents' perception of environmental attributes pertinent to the training situ- ation, including the leadership and instructional styles employed by in- structors, and the fairness and objectivity of grading practices" (James et al., 1980, p. 1).

The scales of the instrument were grouped by statistical procedures (principal components analysis) into five major areas, or dimensions, of psychological climate. The current study has used James et al.'s (1980) PC instrument for that portion of the survey which measures students' psychological perception of their college environment. It used the five dimensions and the designations that define them. The designations given to the five PC dimensions were the following:

Dimension I:	Instructor Support and Facilitation
Dimension II:	Fairness, Objectivity, and Equity of Treatment of Students
Dimension III:	Challenge and Overload
Dimension IV:	Control and Structure
Dimension V:	Competition Among Students.

Along with the assessment of students' psychological climate per- ceptions of the college, the subsequent part of the questionnaire, using items adopted from research conducted by Michele Cisco-Titi (1990), assessed students' perceptions of the extent of social interactions among ten paired student ethnic groups in and outside of the classroom. Four pairs reflected intra-ethnic interaction. The part that follows comprised one item that assessed students' perception of the level of success of Af- rican-American, Asian-American, Hispanic Americans, and White Ameri- can students at the college. The item in another part assessed students' personal inter-ethnic relations at the college; the same four ethnic groups were used along with a specification of any other ethnic groups that was not included.

The final two parts assessed the existence of pride students have for the college, measured by 12 items and students' general satisfaction with the college, measured by 17 items. These sections were researcher-designed with reliance on some items used in the psychological climate(PC) instrument employed in the study conducted by the Institute of Behavioral Research (1980).

All items were measured using Likert-type scales. The psychological climate part of the survey used Likert-type scales that measure agreement/disagreement with questions, the extent of occurrences and frequency of occurrences. Part 11 employed Likert-type scales that measured the extent of interaction between ethnic groups of students. The Likert-type scales in the third part measured the extent of success of the different student ethnic groups. The fourth part determined the existence of pride in the college with a Likert-type scale measuring responses on a "definitely yes" to "definitely no" continuum. The final part employs a Likert-type scale that measured the level of satisfaction/dissatisfaction with the college in general.

Statistical Analysis

All data were analyzed by the Statistical Package for the Social Sciences (SPSS-X). This system is a comprehensive tool for managing, analyzing, and displaying information. As written in SPSSX inc. (1988), "It brings together data management, report writing, and statistical analysis in one comprehensive system with a single language" (p. 1).

Psychological climate (PC) perceptions

Psychological climate scales were measured by 101 items on Likert-type scales, ranging from 1 to 5 with 1 being "not at all," "strongly disagree" or "never" and 5 being "to a great extent," "strongly agree" and "always."

Questions were worded both negatively and positively; consequently, items had to be reverse coded to ensure a sufficiently high reliability coefficient on the scales. An Analysis of Variance (ANOVA) calculated means and counts for the response ratings on each of the scales for groups defined by each biographical factor.

The response ratings on each scale was subsequently subjected to a two-way analysis of variance. Cell means and counts were calculated for each scale in a two-way interaction with groups defined by each biographical factor and ethnicity as defined by three groups (African-American, Hispanic American, and White American). This determined the mean differences in the psychological climate perceptions scales between African-American, Hispanic American, and White American students within groups as defined by the biographical factors.

A procedure Oneway, using the Scheffe procedure, was performed on each scale with ethnic groups to determine if there were significant differences between any of the groups at the .05 level. To determine if there were differences within groups, biographical data were recoded into two groups and subjected to a two-tailed t-test. Ratings for each scale were subjected to a two-tailed t-test for independent samples of gender.

Perceived inter-ethnic group social interactions

A Likert-type scale was employed to determine students' perceived extent of social interactions between pairs of ethnically different students on campus. The scale ranged from 1 to 5 with 1 representing "very limited interaction" and 5 representing "very extensive interaction." The items which measured the scales in this section were subjected to the same statistical analysis procedure as the psychological climate items. Cell means and counts were determined for biographical factors and ethnicity for these items by subjecting them to T-tests, ANOVA and Oneway procedures.

Perceived success of ethnic student groups

The respondents were asked to rate the level of success of each of these groups on campus, using a Likert-type scale that ranged from 1 to 5. One denoted "very unsuccessful" and 5 denoted "very successful." This item was subjected to the same statistical analysis performed on the previous scales.

Personal student inter-ethnic interactions

The respondent's task in this item was to put a check mark against the ethnic group(s) to which most of his/her friends on the campus belonged. To determine a pattern of inter-ethnic relationships for each group of Latin American, African American, and White American students, the responses on this item were subjected to a crosstabulation procedure.

College pride

The 12 items that measured the college pride scale were measured by a Likert-type scale ranging from 1 to 5. One was "definitely not" and 5 was "definitely yes." This scale was subjected to the same statistical manipulations as were the first three sections of the survey. T-tests, ANOVA and Oneway procedures were performed to determine if there were any significant differences in college pride among and within the three ethnic groups and among any groups of the independent biographical factors. To determine the overall effects of all the variables on students' pride in college, this scale was consequently treated as an dependent variable and subjected to a stepwise, backward, regression analysis.

Satisfaction with college

The final 17 items measuring the extent of general satisfaction with college required students to reflect their level of satisfaction on a Likert-type scale ranging from 1 to 5, with 1 being "very dissatisfied" and 5 being "very satisfied." This scale was also subjected to the same statistical manipulations as was the former scale. ANOVA, Oneway, and the two-tailed T-tests were all performed on this scale to assess the extent of satisfaction that each of the ethnic groups experience with the college. Also, they were executed to determine if there are any significant differences of level of satisfaction with the college experienced among and within the three ethnic groups at the .05 level.

To determine the overall effects of all the variables on the level of satisfaction students experience with the college in general, this scale treated as a dependent variable was consequently subjected to a stepwise, backward, regression analysis procedure.

Biographical data

To determine the percentages of White American, African-American, and Latin American students who made up the different groups of biographical factors, it was necessary to perform a crosstabulation procedure on ethnicity and gender, ethnicity and area in which student was raised, ethnicity and type and location of high school student attended respectively, and ethnicity and level of family gross combined income. This procedure allowed for a more in-depth description/background of the three ethnic student groups.

Research Results

Reliability and Frequency Scores for Scales for Student Samples

The reliabilities of the scales were estimated based on the coefficient alphas. The results, as shown in Table 5.3, reflect that all but four scales have a reliability score of .60 and above. The four scales, their reliability scores and the number of items in the scales are (1) psychological influence .531 (4 items); (2) goal emphasis .550 (3 items); (3) academic counseling .551 (3 items); (4) competition .558 (3 items).

Table 5.4 illustrates the frequencies of responses to the scales by the total student sample. The table reports, in the first column, the scale name; in the second column, the mean scores (x); in the third column, the mode score (MO); in column four, the standard deviation (SD); in column five, the median (MDN) for each scale. Column six reports the sample size (N) and the range of the scores, including the minimum and maximum scores (min-max scores) which are reported in the last column.

Research Question #1

Do psychological climate (PC) perceptions vary among African-American, Latin American and White American students?

Psychological climate (PC) perceptions vary significantly between African-American and White American students with respect to (1) interaction-facilitation by instructors; (2) cooperation, friendliness, harmony and trust among students in the college; (3) competition among students in the college; and (4) relationships among students in the college.

Psychological climate (PC) perceptions vary significantly between Latin American and White students with regards to cooperation, friendliness, harmony, and trust among students in the college. There were no significant differences in psychological climate (PC) perceptions between African-American and Latin American students.

Findings

Scale means and standard deviations were compared for each ethnic group to determine if there were significant differences at $p < .05$ among the groups. Differences were found in six of the scales, including 4 of the 21 PC perception scales and "pride in college" and "satisfaction with college." They are: (1) "Inter 2" (interaction facilitation by instructors);

Scale	Number of Items	Reliability Coefficient
1. Instructor Support	8 items	.766
2. Interaction Facilitation	2 items	.579
3. Psychological Influence	4 items	.531
4. Classroom Participation	3 items	.608
5. Instructor Style	4 items	.600
6. Goal Emphasis	3 items	.550
7. General Support	8 items	.760
8. Academic Counseling	3 items	.551
9. Class Cooperation	5 items	.794
10. Fairness	4 items	.576
11. Management Awareness	6 items	.639
12. Equity of Treatment	7 items	.790
13. Role Overload	4 items	.652
14. Competition	3 items	.558
15. Student Relations	7 items	.762
16. Cliqueness Among Students	11 items	.787
17. NonAcademic Counseling	4 items	.647
18. Group Interaction	18 items	.851
19. Success	4 items	.649
20. Pride in College	12 items	.904
21. Satisfaction with College	17 items	.881

Table 5.3: Reliability Scores for Scales for Student Samples

SCALE	X	MO.	SD	MDN	N=	RANGE	(MIN-MAX) SCORE
SUPPORT 1	26.27	27.00	3.54	26.00	249	19	(17-36)
INTER 2	5.52	6.00	1.58	6.00	249	7	(2-9)
INFLU 3	12.15	12.00	1.90	12.00	249	11	(7-18)
PARTIC 4	8.45	9.00	2.08	9.00	249	11	(3-14)
STYLE 5	12.86	13.00	1.85	13.00	249	11	(7-18)
GOAL 6	10.20	12.00	2.06	10.00	2.49	12	(3-15)
GENSUPP 7	25.71	27.00	4.50	26.00	249	28	(12-40)
CONSEL 8	8.56	0.00	1.39	9.00	249	8	(5-13)
COOPER 9	14.87	17.00	3.52	16.00	249	17	(5-22)
FAIRN 10	12.71	13.00	2.08	13.00	249	13	(7-20)
EQUITY 12	21.43	21.00	2.59	21.00	249	16	(12-28)
OVERLO 14	13.72	16.00	2.75	14.00	249	14	(6-20)
COMPET 17	9.04	9.00	1.42	9.00	249	10	(3-13)
STUREL 18	21.94	25.00	3.66	22.00	249	18	(12-30)
CLIQUE 19	36.17	36.00	3.66	36.00	249	30	(21-51)
NACOUN 20	12.81	12.00	1.36	13.00	249	9	(8-17)
GRINTE 21	61.75	70.00	9.53	63.00	249	64	(19-83)
PRIDE 24	41.74	46.00	8.45	43.00	249	46	(14-60)
SATISF 25	58.41	58.00	9.06	59.00	249	49	(34-83)

Table 5.4: Frequency of Scales for Student Sample

(2) "Cooper 9" (class cooperation and friendliness); (3) "Compet 9" (competition among students); (4) "Sturel 18" (student relationships/interactions); (5) "Pride 24" (pride in college); (6) "Satisf 25" (satisfaction with college). The results are illustrated in tables 5.5a and 5.5b.

Significant differences were found between African-Americans and White Americans in their perceptions of "interaction facilitation" or the degree to which they perceived their instructors as encouraging cooperative and harmonious relationships among students. White American students perceived significantly more interaction facilitation (x =5.9) and (SD =1.3) than African -American students (x= 5.1) and (SD=1.7) at p < .05.

The degree of perceived "class cooperation" or cooperativeness, friendly relations, trust, and group spirit among students in classes was significantly different between both White American students and African-American students and White American students and Latin American students. White American students perceived a higher degree of class cooperation (x=16.1) and (SD=2.8), than Latin American student, (x=14.5) and (SD=3.3), and African-American students perceived the least degree of class cooperativeness, (x=13.7) and (SD=3.8). The differences were significant at p < .05. White American students perceived a smaller degree of "competition" among students or pressure to compete with other students for high grades and recognition, (x=8.74) and (SD=1.2), than do African-American students, (x=9.24) and (SD=1.5). This difference is significant at p < .05.

The degree of "pride" that White American and Latin American students have in the college was significantly different than that of African-American students at p < .05, with Latin American students experiencing most pride, (x=43.7) and (SD=7.1). White American students have significantly more pride in the college, (x=42.6) and (SD=8.4), than African-Americans, (x=39.7) and (SD=8.7). Latin American students (x=43.7) have significantly more pride in the college than African-American students (x= 39.7).

The study found a significant difference in degree of "satisfaction" with college between African-American students and Latin American students at p < .05. Latin American students experience the most satisfaction with college in the three groups (x=60.4) and (SD=9.4), while African-American students experience the least satisfaction, (x=56.4) and (SD=10.0).

Student Relations is defined as the extent of perceived social interaction among pairs of ethnically different students groups in and out of the classroom. White Americans perceive significantly more interactions in

SCALE	GROUP 1 (N=98) AFRICAN AMERICANS		GROUP2 (N=53) LATIN AMERICANS		GROUP 3 (N=98) WHITE AMERICANS		F-TEST	SIGNIF. DIFRNT GROUP
	X	SD	X	SD	X	SD		
SUPPORT 1	26.26	3.4	26.61	3.9	25.61	3.3	0.05	NONE
INTER 2	5.11	1.7	5.52	1.4	5.92	1.3	0.00	3/1
INFLU 3	12.02	2.0	11.98	1.5	12.36	1.9	0.34	NONE
PARTIC 4	8.38	2.3	8.67	2.2	8.39	1.7	0.67	NONE
STYLE 5	12.83	2.0	13.00	1.5	12.81	1.7	0.83	NONE
GOAL 6	10.35	2.2	10.28	1.8	10.01	1.9	0.47	NONE
GENSUPP 7	26.29	4.5	25.96	4.5	24.98	4.3	0.11	NONE
COUNSEL 8	8.37	1.4	8.60	1.3	8.73	1.3	0.19	NONE
COOPER 9	13.73	3.8	14.54	3.3	16.19	2.8	0.00	3/1; 3/2
FAIRN 10	12.88	2.0	12.39	2.0	12.70	2.1	0.38	NONE
EQUITY 12	21.17	2.9	21.20	2.4	21.80	2.2	0.18	NONE

Figure 5.5a: Mean Comparison of Psychological Climate (PC) Perception for African-American, Latin-American and White American Student Samples. NOTE: Scheffe Procedure at .05p

SCALE	GROUP 1 (N=98) AFRICAN AMERICANS		GROUP2 (N=53) LATIN AMERICANS		GROUP 3 (N=98) WHITE AMERICANS		F-TEST	SIGNIF. DIFRNT GROUP
	X	SD	X	SD	X	SD		
OVERLO 14	13.79	2.7	13.77	3.0	13.62	2.6	0.89	NONE
COMPET 14	9.24	1.5	9.20	1.3	8.74	1.2	0.02	NONE
STUREL 18	21.23	3.9	21.88	3.6	22.68	3.1	0.02	3/1
CLIQUE 19	36.36	3.8	36.66	3.2	35.71	3.6	0.25	NONE
NACOUN 20	12.84	1.4	12.96	1.4	12.69	1.2	0.48	NONE
GRINTE 21	61.35	11.0	61.19	8.1	62.44	8.5	0.65	NONE
SUCCES 22	14.65	2.3	14.69	1.7	14.28	2.0	0.36	NONE
PRIDE 24	39.73	8.7	43.73	7.1	42.67	8.4	0.00	3/1; 2/1
SATISF 25	56.44	10.0	60.41	9.4	59.3	7.4	0.01	2/1

Table 5.5b: Mean Comparison of Psychological Climate (PC) Perception for African-American, Latin-American and White American Student Samples. NOTE: Scheffe Procedure at .05p

and out of classrooms among pairs of ethnically different students, (x=22.6) and (SD=3.1), than African-American students (x=21.2) and (SD=3.9). The differences are significant at p < .05.

In sum, the study found that among the three ethnic student groups who perceived these six scales significantly different at p < .05, the African-American students have the most negative PC perceptions in all but one scale, the support from instructors, and are least proud of and satisfied with the college. White American students have the most positive perception in all but one PC perception scale, support from instructors, while (a) pride in college and (b) satisfaction in college were perceived most positively by the Latin American students.

Research Question #2

Do psychological climate (PC) perceptions vary among African-American students, Latin American students, and White American students with regard to (1) the type of high school they attended, (2) the location of the high school they attended, (3) their country of birth, (4) the country of their parents' birth, and (5) their gender?

Significant differences in PC perception scales at p < .05 were found existing within each of the three ethnic student groups. The study assesses these differences in relation to five of the biographical items that help to define the ethnicity of the student. They are (1) type of high school attended, (2) location of high school attended, (3) country of birth, (4) country of parents' birth. The item (5) gender was also included as a subgroup.

Psychological climate (PC) perceptions of (a) academic counseling, (b) competition among students, and (c) equity in treatment of all students by instructors varied among African-American students with regards to (1) the location of the high school they attended, (2) their country of birth, and (3) the country of their parents' birth.

Psychological climate (PC) perceptions of (a) fairness in instructors' treatment of all students, (b) student relations, (c) competition among students in the college, (d) academic counseling, (e) equity in treatment of all students by instructors, (f) psychological influence on instructors, and (g) cliqueness among students in college varied among Latin American students. The subgroups within which these significant differences occur are (a) location of high school attended, (b) type of high school attended, (c) student's country of birth, and (d) parents' country of birth.

Psychological climate (PC) perception of (a) academic counseling,

(b) success of the ethnic groups within the college varied among White American students with regards to (a) location of high school attended and (b) gender.

Findings

Most of the significant differences in PC perception were found within the Latin American student sample while the least significant differences exist within the White American student sample. Tables 5.6, 5.7 and 5.8 illustrate the significant differences in PC perception found within each of the three ethnic groups of students.

(A) PC perception differences among African-American students

African-American students differed significantly in their PC perception of (1) academic counseling; (2) competition among students; and (3) equity in treatment of all students by college. These differences were attributed to the subgroups: (a) location of high school attended, (b) country of birth, and (c) parents' country of birth as illustrated in table 5.6.

At p< .05, African-American students do not differ significantly in PC perceptions with respect to the type of high schools that they attended. Students who attended or did not attend public schools do not perceive PC scales significantly different. However, African-American students who attended or did not attend high school in an urban area significantly differ in their PC perception of academic counseling (Sign. P=.026) and their PC perception of competition among students (Sign. P=.010). Students who did not attend high school in an urban area have a more positive perception of academic counseling (x=8.6) than those who attended high school in an urban area (x=8.0). Students whose high schools were located in an urban area perceive more competition among students (x=9.6) than those whose high schools were not in urban areas (x=8.8).

African-American students who were born in the United States differ significantly at p<.05 in one PC perception scale from those who were not born in the US: equity in treatment of all students by the college (sign. p=.026) Students who were not born in the US perceive less equity in treatment by the college of all students irrespective of sex, ethnicity, personality, or regional origin (x=19.5) than did those students born in the US (x=21.4).

The PC perception of equity in treatment of all students by the college is again a source of significant difference within the sample of African-American students whose parents were born and whose parents were

	hs not urb		**hs**	**urb**	
	X	SD	X	SD	Sign. P
Counsel 8	8.6	1.3	8.0	1.4	.026
Compet 17	8.8	1.5	9.6	1.4	.010

	not born US		**born**	**US**	
Equity 12	X	SD	X	SD	Sign. P
	19.5	3.4	21.4	2.7	.021

	P not US		**P**	**US**	
Equity 12	X	SD	X	SD	Sign. P
	19.7	3.4	21.6	2.6	.008

Table 5.6: T-Test Scores for Psychological Climate
Perception:Differences in PC Perception among African-
American Students

	hs not pub		hs	pub	
	X	S	X	SD	Sign. P
Fairn 10	12.8	1.7	11.5	2.1	.026
Sturel 18	21.8	3.8	23.4	2.8	.017

	hs no urb		hs	urb	
	X	SD	X	SD	Sign. P
Compet 17	9.5	1.4	8.8	1.1	.047

	not born US		born	US	
	X	SD	X	SD	Sign. P
Counsel 8	8.2	1.5	8.9	1.0	.045
Equity 12	20.2	2.3	22.1	2.1	.003

	P not US		P	US	
	X	SD	X	SD	Sign. P
Influ 2	11.8	1.5	13.1	.7	.040
Partic 4	8.4	2.2	10.3	1.5	.050
Clique 19	36.3	3.2	39.3	2.4	.033

	not fem		fem		
	X	SD	X	SD	Sign. P
Cooper 9	15.6	3.0	13.7	3.3	.034
Overlo 14	12.8	2.8	14.4	3.0	.055

Table 5.7: T-Test Scores for Psychological Climate Perception:Differences in PC Perception among Latin-American Students

	hs not urb		hs	urb	
	X	SD	X	SD	Sign. P
Counsel 8	8.6	1.3	9.4	1.1	.040

Table 5.8: T-Test Scores for Psychological Climate Perception:Differences in PC Perception among White American Students

not born in the US (sign. P=.008). Students whose parents were not born in the US perceive less equity in treatment by the college of all students (x=19.7) than those whose parents were born in the US (x=21.6). No significant differences in PC perceptions were found between male and female African-American students.

(B) PC perception differences among Latin American students

Latin American students differed significantly in 11 PC perceptions: (1) fairness in treatment of all students by college, (2) student relation/ interaction, (3) competition among students, (4) academic counseling, (5) equity in treatment of all students by college, (6) psychological influence, (7) opportunity for classroom participation, (8) cliqueness of students, (9) support by instructors, (10) student cooperation and friendliness, and (11) overload. These differences are attributed to all the subgroups: (a) location of high school attended, (b) type of high school attended, (c) country of birth, (d) country of parents' birth, and (e) gender of student. Table 5.7 illustrates the mean score (x) and standard deviation (SD) of the PC scale for each subgroup and the t-stat. and the sign. P score for each PC scale.

The study found a significant difference in PC perception of Fairness (sign.P= .026) and student relations/interaction (sign. P=.017) between students who attended and those who did not attend public high schools. Students who did not attend public high schools perceive significantly more fairness in treatment by the college (x=12.8) than those who did attend public high schools (x=11.5) and significantly less interactions among ethnically different pairs of student groups (x=21.0) than those students who did attend public high schools (x=23.4).

The PC perception of competition among students is significantly different (sign. P=.047) between students who attended high schools in urban areas and those who did not. Students who did not attend urban high schools perceived more competition among students (x=9.5) than those who attended urban high schools (x=8.8).

PC perception of academic counseling and equity are significantly different (sign. p< .05, and .003) respectively between Latin American students born in the US and those not born in the US. Students born in the US have more positive feelings about academic counseling (x=8.9) than students not born in the US (x=8.20). Of all students, Latin American students not born in the US, like the African-American students in the same subgroups perceive less equity in treatment by the college (x=20.2) than those student born in the US (x=22.1).

There are significant differences in PC perception in (1) psychological influence (sign. p=.040); (2) opportunity for classroom participation (sign.P=.050); and (3) cliqueness among students (Sign. P=.033) among Latin American students whose parents were born and were not born in the US. Those students whose parents were not born in the US perceive that they have a smaller degree of psychological influence, that is, influence on decisions made by instructors (x=11.8) than those born in the US (x=13.1). Students whose parents were not born in the US perceive less participation or encouragement to participate in classroom discussions (x=8.4) than their counterparts whose parent were born in the US (x=10.3). Students whose parents were not born in the US found a smaller degree of cliqueness among students (x=36.3) than students whose parents were born in the US (x=39.2). Conclusively, Latin American students whose parents were not born in the US perceive a smaller degree of psychological influence, participation and cliqueness than those students whose parents were born in the US.

Significant differences in PC perception of support from instructors (sign.P=.051), cooperation and friendliness among students (sign.P=.034) and overload (sign.P=.055) exist between male and female Latin American students. Latin American male students perceive more "support" from instructors (x=27.8) than do females (x=25.6). They also perceive more cooperation and friendliness among students (x=15.6) than do the female students (x=13.7). However, males perceive less of an overload in course work (x=12.8) than do their female counterparts (x=14.6).

PC perception differences among Euro- American students

The White American student sample, as illustrated in table 5.8, differs significantly in only one PC scale: academic counseling. The subgroup that accounted for this difference is location of high school.

There is a significant difference in PC perception of academic counseling (sign. p=.026) between white students who attended high school in an urban area and those who did not. Those students who attended urban high schools have a more positive perception of academic counseling (x=9.4) than those who did not. No significant differences were found within the White American student subgroups of (a) type of high school attended and (b) gender.

General observations

Of the three respondent groups, Latin Americans had the most significant differences in PC perceptions of the college within their group. Each of the five subgroups accounted for the variability in perception differences within that ethnic group. The significant differences in PC perceptions among African-American students were accounted for by three of the five subgroups. White American students differed significantly in only one PC perception scale accounted for by one out of the five subgroups. It is important to note here that the sample size for two of the five subgroups among the White American respondents was significantly small: (1) students born out of the US among White Americans (n=2) and (2) parents born out of the US (n=2). The sample size of these two subgroups was too small to yield any significant results, so it was consequently thrown out of the student sample for this procedure.

Research Question #3

Is there a relationship between students' ethnicity, their psychological climate (PC) perception and concomitant satisfaction with the college?

The results of the statistical analyses in this section answer the question: What is the relationship between satisfaction in college and PC perception and biographical characteristics of (a) the total student sample; (b) the African-American student sample, (c) the Latin American student sample, and (d) the White American student sample?

There is a moderately strong relation between African-American students' psychological climate (PC) perception of four aspects of the environment and their satisfaction with the college. There is a significantly strong relationship between Latin American students' psychological climate perceptions of four aspects of the environment and their satisfaction with the college. There is a moderately strong relationship between White American students' psychological climate (PC) perception of 10 aspects of the environment and their satisfaction with the college.

Findings

Final variables in the equation for the total student sample

Following a backward elimination entry procedure for the total student sample there were nine variables left in the equation. They accounted for 53% of the variability of satisfaction with college (R^2=.53727). The regression of satisfaction with college on variables that have the most impact on satisfaction (F-stat=26.318) is very significant. Table 5.9 illustrates the results.

Predictor	B	BETA	T-STAT.	<P
Counsel 8	-0.77	-0.11	-2.41	.016
hs not pub	-1.87	-0.09	-1.91	.057
Compet 17	0.66	0.10	2.12	.034
Sturel 18	0.86	0.35	6.62	.000
Grinte 21	0.14	0.14	2.94	.003
Fairn 10	-0.68	0.15	-3.15	.001
Ethn	0.83	0.12	2.37	.018
Inter	0.62	0.10	1.89	.059
Support 1	0.94	0.36	6.77	.000
(CONSTANT)	10.965614	1.677		.0950

R=.53727 F-STAT=26.3181 ADJ.R=.51686 SIGN-F=.00 DF=9

Table 5.9: Final Variables in Relationship Between Satisfaction with College and Psychological Climate (PC) Perception and Biographical Dimensions.

The independent variables with the highest degree of impact on the dependent variable (satisfaction with college) are: (1) Counsel8 (beta=-.11) (<P=.016); (2) HSnoturb (beta=-.09)(<P=.057); (3) Compet17 (beta=.10)(<P=.034); (4) StuRel18 (beta=.35)(<P=.000); (5) GrInte21 (beta=.14)(<P=.003); (6) Fairn10 (beta=-.15)(<P=.001); (7) Ethn (beta=.12)(<P=.018); (8) Inter2 (beta=.10)(<P=.059); (9) Support1 (beta=.36)(<P=.000).

Comparison of the relationship between satisfaction with college and PC perceptions and biographical characteristics for African-American, Latin-American and White American student.

With a backward elimination entry procedure employed (see Table 5.10), the results for the three respondent groups show that there are five predictors for satisfaction with college for the African-American student sample, four predictors for the Latin American student sample and 11 predictors for White American students satisfaction with college. However, the regressions on satisfaction of the predictors for the African-American (F-stat=22.0) and Latin American (F-stat.=28.8) student samples were higher than that of the White American student sample (F-stat.=12.3).

The 4 predictors for the Latin American sample account for a significant 75% of the variability within the sample's satisfaction with college, while for the White American student sample, 11 predictors account for 63%, and the 5 African-American student sample predictors account for 59%. Of the 3 student samples, the predictors for the Latin American respondent group have the highest regression on and account for the most variability of the dependent variable, satisfaction with college.

Although there are predictors that are shared between groups within the three respondent groups, the degree of the relationships of the predictors with satisfaction with college differs between the groups. Student relations account for 44% of the variability in satisfaction for African-American students (beta=.44) and 24% of the variability for Latin American students (beta=.24). The relationships for both groups are significant (<P=.00) and (<)=.01) respectively.

Academic counseling accounts for 21% of variability in a negative relationship with satisfaction for African-Americans (beta=-.21) and 16% of the variability for White American students in a negative relationship with satisfaction (beta=-.16). The relationships between the variables for the two groups are significant ,with the African-American (<P=.00) relationship being more significant than the White American sample (<P=.02).

General support from college accounts for 34% of the variability in satisfaction for African-American students (beta=.34) in a positive relationship while it accounts for 44% of the variability in a negative relationship with satisfaction for White American students (beta=-.44). Although both relationships are significant at <P=.00, the directions of the relationship between the two groups make the differences very significant. The more general support that African-American students perceive, the more satisfied they are with the college. On the other hand, the more

PREDICTOR	AFRICAN AMERICAN		LATIN AMERICAN		WHITE AMERICAN	
	BETA	<P	BETA	<P	BETA	<P
STUREL18	0.44	0.00	0.24	0.01	-0.16	0.02
COUNSEL 8	-0.28	0.00			-0.44	0.00
GENSUPP 7	0.34	0.00			0.71	0.00
SUPPORT 1			0.28	0.01		
HSNOTPUB	-0.14	0.05				
GRINTE 21	0.34	0.00				
FAIRN 10			-0.20	0.02	-0.15	0.04
GOAL			0.40	0.00		
SUCCES 22					0.18	0.01
NACOUN 20					0.19	0.01
INCOME					-0.30	0.00
OVERFLO 14					-0.17	0.02
COMPET 17					0.23	0.00
INTER 2					0.16	0.06
PARTIC 4					0.15	0.07
R^2	0.59217		0.75692		0.63541	
ADJ. R^2	0.56534		0.73064		0.58400	
F-STAT	22.07022		28.80318		12.35818	
SIGN-F	0.000		0.00		0.00	
DF	5.00		4.00		11.00	

Table 5.10: Comparison of the Relationship Between Satisfaction with College and Psychological Climate (PC) Perceptions and Biographical Dimensions.

general support that White American students perceive, the less satisfied they are with the college.

Support from instructors accounts for 28% of the variability in the relationship with satisfaction for Latin American students (beta=.28). It accounts for a significant 71% of the variability in satisfaction for White American students (beta=.71). The relationships are significant for both groups, with White American students having a more significant relationship (<P=.00) than Latin American students (<P=.01).

Fairness of treatment of all students by the college accounts for 20% of the variability in a negative relationship with satisfaction for Latin American students (beta=-.20), while it accounts for 15% of variability for White American students (beta=-.15). The relationships between the two variables for both samples, Latin Americans (<P=.02) and White American (<P=.04) are moderately significant.

Summary

The three respondent groups differ significantly in perception of that aspect of the environment which addresses relationships among students. The most significant differences occur between African-American and White American students with White Americans having a more positive perception of all the respective variables. The Latin American respondents are more proud of and satisfied with the college than are African-American and White American students, while African-American students are the least proud of or satisfied with the college than the other two groups. There are significant differences in perception within each of the ethnic groups with most of the differences occurring with the Latin American student group.

The predictors for the African-American sample totalled 59% of the variability of satisfaction. The Latin American student sample totalled 75% while the variability of satisfaction for the White American students totalled 63%.

Those African-American students who did not attend public high schools, those who perceived more relationships between students, more general support of students from the college, and more group interactions among all students were more satisfied with college. The more positively academic counseling was perceived, the less satisfied were respondents from this student sample.

Those Latin American students who perceived more relationships among students, more clarity of instructor's goals, and more support from instructors were more satisfied with the college. However, the more fairness of treatment all students perceived, the less satisfied they are with the college.

White American students' satisfaction with college is influenced by positive perceptions of success, high competition among students, more positive non-academic counseling, more interaction-facilitation by instructors, greater support by instructors, and more opportunity to participate in class. However, the more supportive and fair they perceive instructors to be of all students, the heavier they perceive their workload to be. Also, the higher their family incomes, and the more positively they perceive academic counseling, the less satisfied they are with college.

CHAPTER 6

Social Cognition of Ethnic Groups in College Climate: Implications of Experimental Survey Results

One of the central questions addressed in this study was whether psychological climate (PC) perceptions varied as a result of differences in ethnicity among college students. Ethnicity, in this aspect of the study, is viewed from Samovar and Porter's (1991) perspective, which suggests that it is a result of the geographic origin of the minorities in a country or culture. However, because of the nature of the research question under investigation, ethnicity is used not only with respect to the minority African-American and Latin American student groups, but also with respect to the dominant White American cultural group. The members of the three student groups were defined by geographical origins: African-Americans are students whose foreparents originated from the continent of Africa; Latin Americans students migrated from Latin American countries, while White Americans students have their roots in the European continent.

This chapter presents a discussion of the implications of the survey results for the following research questions: (1) Do psychological climate (PC) perception vary among African American, Latin American, and White American students; and (2) Do psychological climate (PC) perceptions vary among African-American students, Latin American students and White American students with regard to (a) the type of high school they attended, (b) the location of the high school they attended, (c) their country of birth, the country of their parents' birth, and (d) their gender? It then discusses the results and implications of the research question: (3) Is there a relationship between students' ethnicity, their psychological climate (PC) perceptions and concomitant satisfaction with college?

Theoretical Implications of the Differences in Psychological Climate (PC) Perception Among Ethnically different Student Groups

PC perception differences among ethnic student groups

Significant differences in perception were found in 6 of the 21 scales: (1) interaction facilitation by Instructor, (2) class cooperation and friendliness, (3) competition among students, (4) student relations outside of classroom, (5) pride in college, and (6) satisfaction with college. Although there are not significant differences among all three respondent groups in each of these 6 scales, significant differences were found between African-American students and Latin American students, African-American and White American students, and White American and Latin American student groups.

PC perception differences between African-American and White American students

There are significant differences in perception between African-American students and White American students in five of the 6 scales in which significant differences in perception exist. African-American students perceive a significantly less degree of "interaction facilitation by instructors" than do White American students. They also perceive significantly less "cooperation and friendliness among students" than do white American students who perceive a significantly less amount of "competition among students" than they do. The extent of "student relations outside of class" is perceived as significantly less by African-American students than by White American students. African-American students are significantly less "proud of the college" than are White American students.

This trend in the differences in PC perception between these two ethnic groups suggests that they function within a college climate in which relationships among students are perceived by African-American students to be significantly less cooperative, harmonious, trusting, and friendly and significantly more competitive than they are perceived by their White American colleagues who are significantly more proud of their college than they are. However, these two respondent ethnic groups do not have significantly different psychological climate (PC) perception of the other aspects of the college environment. This finding is consistent with those of Astin (1982) and Cheatham et. al (1986). These investigators, following a review of the literature that examines university climate perceptions, concluded that there exists a shift from relatively divergent perceptual experiences between black and white university students to the sharing by these groups of relatively similar perceptions of campus ambience and institutional policies. They also seem to share similar academic and career goals.

The significant differences in perception between African-American and White American students within those scales that relate to the climate of student relationships in the environment indicate, according to the psychological climate (PC) theory, indicate that these two groups use different information processing and cognitive filtering processes to come to significantly different perceptions of the same phenomenon in the college climate. However, the other probable reasons for the lack of perceptual agreement in this aspect of the college environment cannot be ignored. According to James et al. (1978) and Schneider (1975), the significant differences in perceptual agreement in this dimension of the college environment can also be explained by the likelihood that students in the same college environment might not be exposed to the same set of situational attributes and events. In other words, there is the likelihood that these perceptions of the climate of student relationships were drawn from students with whom these responding ethnic groups tended to interact. It is important to note that African-American and White American students may have social relationships with different ethnic groups of students in the college and consequently may not be exposed to the same groups of students from which their perceptions were made. This is likely to result in differences in perceptions in that aspect of the college climate that defines the quality and characteristics of relationships among students in the college.

The second probable reason for the lack of perceptual agreement among these ethnic groups is that if perceptions of these two groups are indeed based on the entire student body, then the likelihood exists that there may be an inherent bias in the "selection" of the ethnic groups from which perceptions are drawn. Because of the predominance of a White American student body, White students' perceptions may be based in general on this population. African-American students, having had more of an opportunity to interact with students from the African-American, Latin American and White American student groups, may tend to base their perceptions on actions of these three ethnic groups on the campus. It is noteworthy that the significant differences in PC perception that do exist between these two groups occur only in the scales that define the perception of the relationship, cooperation, harmony, trust, friendliness, and competition among students in the college. However, PC theory does not offer an explanation for the reason why the significant perceptual differences between these two groups are concentrated in this one aspect of the college environment. This study only speculates that this finding may indicate that relationships among students is that aspect of the college environment, which is most subjected to variance in perception since there are no formal rules that govern behavior or the nature of the relationships between the students.

The study further suggests that the similarity in the two ethnic groups' psychological climate perceptions of the style of and the equity in treatment from, and supportiveness of the predominantly White American teaching staff indicates a possible objectivity in the nature of this aspect of the college environment. Despite certain African-American students' allegations of racism by specific faculty members during informal interviews conducted in this research, the general consensus of the relationship between instructors and students was consistent with the finding mentioned above. This finding does not support the position that African-American and White American students possess different cognitive frames which allow them to perceive situations and events differently; instead, it seems to support the organizational climate position that climate is a characteristic of the organization. The consensus of perception of these aspects of the environment may be as a result of the objective nature of instructors' behavior and the objective nature of academic and non-academic counseling. This objectivity is ensured because consistency in action and equity in treatment of all students are required of educators and administrators at any level. This finding certainly raises questions that might be answered in future research.

PC perception differences between White American and Latin-American students

White American and Latin American students differ significantly in only one of the 6 scales in which there are significant PC perception differences. White American students perceive significantly more "cooperation, trust, and friendliness among students in the college" than Latin American students. Although not significantly so, Latin American students are more "proud" of and "satisfied" with the college than are White American students.

However, it is important to note that although these two respondent groups only differ significantly in one PC perception scale, they do not share very similar perceptions with reference to "competition among students" and "relationships among students outside of class." Latin American students perceive more "competition among students" and less "relationship among students outside of class" than do White American students. According to psychological climate (PC) theory, these two respondent groups, because of differences in ethnicity, employ different cognitive and information processing frames as they perceive the same phenomenon. As a consequence, their perceptions of "cooperation, trust and friendliness among students" are significantly different.

Yet another possible reason for this significant perceptual difference is that the two groups may not be equally exposed to the same groups of students from which this perception developed. If perceptions are based on students' generalizations of situations or events that they are exposed to, according to James et al. (1978) and Schneider (1975), the results of this study that reveal that White American students have more friends within their own ethnic group than either of the other two respondent ethnic groups become important. This implies that they are comfortable with and relate effectively to each other, having little problems with cooperation, trust, and harmony in their relationships with each other. Consequently, they would perceive the relationships positively. The fact that Latin American students, more so than White American students, tend to have friends outside their ethnic group implies that their perception could have evolved from their exposure to more than one ethnic group on campus. As a consequence, it is likely that the two ethnic groups will have differences in perception of this aspect of the college environment. The predominance of a White American student body who function within their own tightly-knit ethnic group on this campus may contribute to White American students holding a significantly more positive perception of the degree of "friendliness, trust, and cooperation among students on campus" than do the Latin American students, some of whom interact outside of their ethnic group.

Again emerges the question of why these two groups differ significantly in this singular PC scale that defines the nature and characteristic of the relationship between students on the campus. Taking into consideration that psychological climate (PC) perceptions are subjective in nature, it may be reasonable to conclude that the other aspects of the college climate, such as academic counseling, instructors' support and style, may not yield to subjective interpretations because objectivity in these areas is ensured by college policies and requirements. The phenomenon of this isolated case of significant perceptual difference between these two ethnic groups can only be understood following further research on the issue.

PC perception differences between Latin-American students and African American students

Latin American and African-American students did not differ significantly in any of the psychological climate (PC) perception scales; however, Latin American students are significantly more "proud" of and "satisfied" with the college than are African-American students.

Results indicate that Latin American and African-American students share almost similar perceptions of the degree of cooperation, trust, friendliness, and competition among students, as well as a similar degree of the relationships among students outside of class. Interestingly, despite this consensuality in perception of this aspect of the college environment, Latin American students function within a college environment that they are significantly more proud of and satisfied with than do African-American students. This finding is particularly interesting to this study as it seems to indicate that the level of pride in and satisfaction with college for these two ethnic groups are not contingent on perceptions of similar aspects of the college environment. Of particular interest is the fact that these two ethnic groups share a history of development as minorities in a society dominated by another ethnic majority and tend to have similar social, family, and economic experiences. Why then would their levels of pride in and satisfaction with the same college be so significantly different, despite their similarities in perceptions of student life?

This similarity in perception, in accordance with PC theory, indicates that African-American and Latin American students share similar cognitive and informational processes that allow them to perceive this phenomenon in an almost similar way. How or if this psychological climate perception relates to their level of satisfaction and pride in college is a research question that will be answered and discussed further in the study.

Implication of Findings

These findings indicate that the most significant differences in perception in the 6 scales occur between African-American students and White American students in five of those scales. African-American students and Latin American students do not differ significantly in perception in any of the psychological climate (PC) scales but certainly experience significant differences in pride in and satisfaction with the college.

These findings also suggest that there is a consensuality in PC perceptions shared by the three respondent groups with reference to the other aspects of the college environment that relate to the degree of instructors' supportiveness, teaching styles, fairness, and equity in treatment. They also seem to share similar perceptions about the degree of academic and non-academic counseling, cliqueness of students with respect to gender, race, and nationality, and the degree of success of each of the three ethnic groups of students. This perceptual agreement implies that there is some objectivity to those aspects of the college environment, as organizational climate theory postulates. These aspects may be governed by formal and informal rules and expectations, such as that dimension of the college environment that pertains to faculty and administrative behavior as well as equal and fair treatment of students.

Along with the significant differences in pride in and satisfaction with the college among the three respondent groups, the significant differences found in PC perceptions suggest that African-American, and to some extent Latin American students, are less satisfied with the quality of relationships, interactions, and trust than are White American students. For example, there are differences in the extent to which instructors are perceived as encouraging cooperative and harmonious relationships among students. Differences exist also in the degree to which there is perceived friendliness, trust, and group spirit among students in classes. There are also differences in the degree of perceived competition among students for high grades and recognition, as well as the degree of perceived relationships among students outside of class. Conclusively, the significant differences in perception are concentrated in the areas of relations, interactions, trust and cooperation among students in the college. This implies that this dimension of the college environment is more prone to subjectivity in perception, since the action and behavior of students toward each other is not governed by expectations and rules.

It is noteworthy that African-American students perceive all four of the PC scales that measure the degrees of students' relationships, interactions, cooperation, trust and friendliness and competition, along with the pride scale significantly more negatively than do White American students. It can be postulated, therefore, that the three fundamentals of cognitive-learning theory and interactional psychology employed by James et al. 1978) to explain PC perception are salient. These fundamentals are that (1) individuals respond primarily to cognitive representations of situations rather than situation per se; (2) these cognitive representations of situations are related to prior experiences and learning, and (3) most human learning is cognitively mediated. James and Sells (1978) have also postulated that individuals who have had different learning experiences develop different cognitive schemas to interpret situations.

Employing this theoretical development to the current study, the implications of the findings are that African-American and White American students possess cognitive schemas, products of their own ethnic developmental experiences that are consequently very different from each other. Because these two groups share dissimilar economic, cultural, and social experiences in the United States, they will inevitably employ their own unique cognitive schemas to interpret events in the college environment. As a consequence, their perception of the degree of student relations, interaction trust, and so on will significantly differ.

There were no significant differences in perception of PC between Latin-American and African-American students. In fact, the degree of perception of the four PC scales was almost similar for these two respondent groups. This implies that Latin American and African-American students may have cognitive schemas that are almost similar. This may be attributed to the similarity in family structure, the importance of relationships to these two ethnic groups, and the similarity in economic and social experiences as minority status groups in a white dominated nation.

Latin American students, like African-American students, significantly differ with White American students in perception of the degree of cooperation, trust, and friendliness that exists among students in the college. Again, this implies an interpretation that is based on a cognitive schema that results from ethnic development. However, although this is the only PC scale on which these two groups significantly differ, as already mentioned, Latin American and African-American students shared almost similar perceptions of all four of the PC scales in which perceptions were significantly different.

As already mentioned, the high incidence of significantly different perceptions in the PC scales that define that aspect of the psychological climate (PC) environment that relates to relations, interactions, competition, and trust among students requires further exploration.

Summary of Implication of PC Perception among Ethnic Groups

Indications of the findings of PC perception differences among the three ethnic groups are that there is a consensuality of PC perceptions among the three ethnic groups as it pertains to the college environment, with the exception of those aspects that define the extent, quality, and character of the relationship between students on the campus. African-American students hold significantly less positive perceptions of student relations on the campus than do White American students and are significantly less proud of and satisfied with the college than are both Latin American and White American students. Although Latin American students are significantly more proud of the college than White Americans and African-Americans and are significantly more satisfied with it than African-Americans, they share similar PC perception with African-Americans about the extent and quality of the relationship among students on the campus, but have a less negative perception of it.

The general implication of these findings is that ethnicity does determine psychological climate (PC) perceptions of those aspects of the environment in which behaviors are unaltered by policies, legislations, and laws. Organizational governance results in a more objective and consistent behavior of the governed. It is then possible that there are aspects of the environment that can be considered characteristic of the organization according to the postulations of the theory of organizational climate. Consequently, perceptions of the behaviors will tend to be consistent and objective. On the other hand, behaviors that are natural and unaltered because of the absence of regulations and policies, tend to be subjected to a wider range of interpretations than those that are not. Interpretations are the result of a perceptual process filtered through cognitive frames which are designed during the individuals' ethnic development as postulated by the theory psychological climate (PC) perception. As a result, ethnically different individuals will perceive subjective aspects of the environment in different ways.

Implications of Psychological Climate (PC) Perception Differences Within African-American, Latin American and White American Student Groups

Significant perceptual differences in PC scales were found within each of the three respondent ethnic groups; however, the least number of differences were found within the White American student group. The findings imply that the Latin American student group is the most heterogeneous among the three ethnic groups since the most significant perceptual differences were found existing within this groups. The White American respondent group is the most homogeneous, with the least amount of significant perceptual differences occurring within this group.

The extent of variations in perception within the groups can be explained by the number of students within each group who attended public high schools versus private or parochial high schools, high schools located in urban versus non-urban areas; those students who were born in the US as opposed to those who were not, those students whose parents were born in the US versus those who were not, and finally, male versus female students. These dimensions, according to Longstreet (1978), constitute the development of ethnicity. There is an apparent correlation between the extent to which these subgroups varied within these respondent groups and the extent of perceptual differences that occur within the groups. For example, Latin American students varied more than African-American and White American groups in relation to all of the subgroups and consequently differed the most in perception among themselves, while White American students varied very little in relation to perception within the group and just as inconsequentially in relation to all the subgroups except for gender and location of high school.

These findings imply that perceptual differences in psychological climate (PC) perception in the college environment within each of the ethnic groups was a result of inter-ethnicity. This implication gives credence to Longstreet's (1978) postulation about the development of ethnicity, one of the theories from which the conceptual framework of this study evolves. An individual's development, according to her, is determined by ethnicity which is that part of culture that is influenced by one's family background, the schools he/she attends and the country in which he/she grows. The Latin American respondent group was the most diverse of the three with regard to country of birth. The majority of African-American and White American students were born in the US while Latin American students were born in the US as well as in a variety of Latin American countries. The study's conceptual framework evolves from the postulation that ethnicity determines perception and would consequently have an impact on psychological climate (PC) perception.

Implications of psychological climate PC differences among African-American students

African-American students do not differ in PC perception with reference to the type of high school that they attended and gender. However, the type of high school they attended; their country of birth; and the country of their parents' birth attributed to the differences in PC perception experienced within the group.

Those African-American students who attended high schools located in urban areas perceived significantly more competition among students at the college and perceived academic counseling significantly more negative than those who did not attend urban high schools. Significantly less equity in treatment of all students by instructors were perceived by African-American students who were not born in the US than those who were and by students whose parents were not born in the US and those who were.

Interestingly, "equity in treatment of students by instructors" is the PC scale common to subgroups of students who were or were not born in the US and those whose parents were or were not born in the US . This implies that students and students' parents who are African-Americans by birth are more comfortable with the treatment from the faculty at the college than are those students or those students whose parents are not African-American by birth as they perceive their treatment by faculty as more equitable.

Implications of the PC differences among White American students

As already mentioned, White American students do not vary much in relation to the subgroups. The only significant differences were in the subgroups that defined type of high school and gender. However, there were no significant differences in PC perception among those White American students who attended and those who did not attend public high schools. White American females perceived that African-American, Asian Americans, Latin American, and White American students were significantly more successful than did White American males.

Although there are a disproportionately smaller number of White American students that attended urban schools than those who did not, those who attended urban schools perceived academic counseling significantly more positively than those White American students who did not attend an urban high school.

In general, there is an insignificant interethnic experience among White American students at the college. Almost all students and their parents were born in the US and almost all of these students did not attend high schools in urban areas. Consequently, this implies that there is no potential for interethnic perceptual PC differences in the college environment.

Implications for PC differences among Latin American students

There is almost an even distribution of Latin American students throughout the subgroups, resulting in a heterogeneity among this interethnic group of students. This consequently implies, in accordance with Longstreet's (1978) theory of ethnicity, that there will be an equally varied difference in PC perception among this respondent group.

Latin American students who attended public high schools perceive significantly less "fairness in treatment of all students by instructors" and significantly more "relationship among students out of class" than do those who did not attend public high schools. Those who attended high schools in urban areas perceive significantly less "competition among students" than those who did not attend high schools in urban areas.

Latin American students who were not born in the US perceive significantly less "equity in treatment of all students by instructors" and have a significantly more negative perception of "academic counseling" than do those who were born in the US. Those students whose parents were not born in the US perceive a significantly less " degree of influence on instructors" and significantly less "opportunity for participation in class" than those students born in the US. Those Latin American students who were not born in the US perceive significantly less "cliqueness among students in the college" than those born in the US.

These findings reveal that Latin American students who were not born in the US and those whose parents were not born in the US perceive equity in treatment of students, academic counseling, students' influence on instructors, and opportunity for classroom participation significantly more negatively than do those Latin American students were born in the US and whose parents were born in the US.

Implications of the Comparison of Interethnic Differences among African-American, Latin-American and White American students

A comparison of the interethnic differences among Latin American students and among African-American students reveals that students from the two ethnic groups who were not born in the US perceive significantly less "equity in treatment of all students by instructors" than do students from their ethnic group who were born in the US. It is noteworthy that unlike this Latin American respondent subgroup, there are no significant differences in perception among the African-American subgroup with reference to "influence on instructors" and "opportunity to participate in class." However, Latin American and African-American students whose parents were not born in the US share the same psychological climate perceptions about the extent of these two aspects of the college environment. African-American respondents born in the US have a more negative perception of these two aspects than Latin American students born in the US.

Yet another comparison reveals that there are significant differences in perceptions of the "degree of competition among students in the college" among Latin American students and among African-American students who attended urban high schools. Latin Americans who attended urban high schools perceive significantly less "competition among students" than those who did not, while African-Americans who attended urban high schools perceive significantly more "competition among students" than those who did not. Interestingly, Latin Americans who attended urban high schools and African-Americans who did not perceive the same extent of "competition among students in the college."

Comparisons of the perceptions of White American students with the other ethnic groups with reference to country of birth and country of parents' birth were not possible because of the insignificant number of White students in these subgroups. However, White American students who attended urban high schools perceive "academic counseling" significantly more positively than those who did not attend urban high schools, while African-American students who attended urban high schools perceive "academic counseling" significantly more negatively than those who did not attend urban high schools. White American respondents, as a whole, perceive this aspect of the college environment more positively than African-American respondents.

These findings about the comparisons of interethnic differences among the three respondent groups indicate that there are no similarities in perception among these three ethnic respondent groups as a result of type and location of high schools and gender. There are, however, similarities between Latin American and African-American students in psychological climate perceptions of certain aspects of the college environment. These similarities are characteristic of those students whose parents were not born in the US. There are also similarities in the PC scales in which there were significant differences in perceptions as a result of the country of birth of students in these two ethnic groups. This implies that the country of students' birth has some influence on their perception of the college environment.

This finding gives credence to Samovar and Porter's theory that the last step in the perceptual process, interpretation and evaluation, is not the same in all people because this step is a learned process influenced primarily by culture. They further explain that the interpretations we make of situations in the environment are individualistic and are representative of a unique set of experiences in the culture in which we were raised.

Inter-ethnicity is defined by Samovar and Porter's assertion (1991) in *Intercultural Communication* as the differences in geographic origins of individuals or groups of individuals who share the same ethnicity. In other words, national differences within an ethnic group become the determinant of Inter-ethnicity. Just over 60% of the Latin American students' parents and approximately 20% of African-American students' parents were not born in the US. Therefore, some differences in perceptions within these two groups are expected, with more differences occurring within the Latin American respondent group.

Each nation is characterized by its own culture; each culture has its unique set of values and beliefs which are key ingredients in the cognitive frames that it provides its nationals. On migration, individuals take with them the learned cultural values which become salient to them as they exist in their adopted countries. It is consequent that the interethnic groups of African-American and especially of Latin American respondents will not share the same perceptions in all aspects of the college environment. Longstreet (1978) suggests that it is the individual's family, scholastic and national ethnicity that determines the development of his/her ethnicity and it is that individual's ethnicity that predisposes him/her to cognize/perceive things in ways that are unique to his/her culture.

Implications of the Relationship Between Students' Ethnicity, their Psychological Climate (PC) Perceptions and Concomitants Satisfaction with College

One interesting result of this study is that despite the findings that Latin American and African-American students share almost similar PC perceptions of all aspects of the college environment, Latin American students are significantly more satisfied with the college than are African-American students. White American students, even though not significantly so, are less satisfied with the college than Latin American students and more satisfied than African-American students. This implies that there is some difference in those aspects of the college environment that are psychologically meaningful to each ethnic group; those aspects would consequently influence students' satisfaction with the college.

The current study's findings of the relationship between satisfaction and PC perception indeed indicate that the PC perception predictors of satisfaction and the strength of the relationships between the predictors and satisfaction for each of the respondents groups are quite varied. These intergroup divergences in satisfaction predictors have an important implication for the present study in that they suggest that there is no intergroup consensuality on dimensions of the college environment that determine satisfaction with the college. This implies a lack of intergroup concurrence on aspects of the environment that are psychologically meaningful.

A comparison of the predictors of satisfaction with college for each respondent group reveals that four PC scales and type of high school attended predict and account for a moderate variability in the level of satisfaction with college for African-American. Four PC scales predict and account for a significant percent of variability in Latin American students' level of satisfaction with college, and 10 PC scales along with level of income predict and account for a moderate percent of variability in the level of satisfaction that White American students experience with college. Of interest to the current study is that "student relations" is the only PC scale that predicts satisfaction for both Latin American and African-American students. "Support from instructors" and "fairness in treatment" are the two PC scales that predict satisfaction for Latin American and White American students. For African-American and White American students, "academic counseling" and "general support by instructors" are the two predictors of satisfaction with college.

Implications of the relationship between satisfaction and PC perception and biographical data for African-American students

Of the five predictors of satisfaction for African-American students, results reveal that those who perceive more general support from instructors, more interactions among ethnic groups, and more positive relationships among students on campus are more satisfied with college than those who do not. On the other hand, those students who attended public high schools are less satisfied with the college than those who did not. Of particular interest is the finding that the more positively African-American students perceive academic counseling, the less satisfied they are with the college. The implication that underlies this finding is important and merits further investigation. Does it relate to the possibility that the college may use academic counseling as the solution to the symptoms of the African-American student's fundamental problems rather than a solution to the causes of the problem? If this is so, then what academic counseling may do in this research setting is to serve as an inadvertent conduit for self dissatisfaction and consequently dissatisfaction with college in general. This finding, however, deserves further investigation.

Taken together, the predictors of satisfaction for African-American students suggest that these students need positive student relations, positive interethnic groups interactions, and support from instructors in order for them to be satisfied with their college. The implication of these findings is that academic counseling contributes to their dissatisfaction with college since it may be the incorrect solution to their problems.

Implications of the relationship between satisfaction and PC perception and biographical data for Latin American students

The four predictors of satisfaction for Latin American students are very strong as they account for a significant percentage of variability in satisfaction. Latin American students who perceive relationships among students, support from instructors, and goal emphasis by instructors in a positive light tend to be more satisfied with the college than those who do not. However, the more fairness and objectivity perceived in performance assessment, the less they are satisfied in college. This is a unique finding which seems to suggest that Latin American students are part of a culture in which personality, favoritism, and reputation, those characteristics that define this PC scale, are used to assess performance within that ethnic group.

In general, goal emphasis and support by instructors, along with positive relationships among students in the college and less fairness in performance assessment, are those predictors that determine the Latin American student's level of satisfaction.

Implications of the relationship between satisfaction and PC perceptions and biographical data for White American students

Interestingly, 10 PC perception scales and a family's income level account for a moderate percentage of the variability of satisfaction for White American students. This implies that the predictability of each of these scales for satisfaction with college for White American students is not as strong as those for African-American and especially for Latin American students. Findings show that "fairness in treatment," "interaction facilitation by instructors," and "opportunity to participate in classroom discussions" are not very strong predictors of satisfaction for respondents of this ethnic group.

The level of perceived success of the ethnic groups, the level of perceived competition among the ethnic groups, the perception of non-academic counseling, the perceived level of interaction facilitation by instructors, the perceived level of support from instructors, and the perceived opportunity for participating in classroom discussions all have a positive effect on the level of satisfaction that White American students experience. In other words, the more positively these aspects of the college climate are perceived, the more satisfied White American students are with the college.

On the other hand, White respondents who have a positive perception of academic counseling tend to be less satisfied with the college. This suggests that these students believe that the need for academic counseling reflects a self-deficiency which determines one's self esteem and, as a result, may affect the student's level of satisfaction with the college. The level of family income in this respondent group is another predictor of satisfaction; the lower the income level of the students' family, the more satisfied they are with the college. This finding implies that levels of expectations are related to levels of satisfaction. Students who enter the college from low economic backgrounds, unlike their more economically fortunate colleagues, may not have a high level of expectations of life at college. They would have achieved satisfaction on simply entering a high-priced, private college which was never within their family budget Therefore, "college life" is not as meaningful to them as it may be to students whose satisfaction is not anchored on entering a high-priced educational institution of this type. White American students who perceive an overload with college courses are less satisfied with college than those who do not. Interestingly, those who perceive more general support from instructors are less satisfied with college than those who perceive less. This finding implies that the more supportive White American students perceive instructors are of all students, the less satisfied they are with the college. It is interesting, however, that they are generally more satisfied if they perceive that instructors are supportive of them on an individual basis.

These findings of the relationship between PC perceptions and satisfaction with college for the three respondent groups have important implications for the study of PC perception of ethnically different organizational members of their working/college environments. The findings indicate that African-American, Latin-American, and White American students in this research setting have divergent combinations of factors that determine their satisfaction level with the college. The implication, consequently, is that ethnicity is a determinant of what aspects of the organizational environment become meaningful to the individual.

CHAPTER 7

Implications of Survey Results for the Quest for Organizational Diversity

The findings of this study in this communication setting offers some understand of the status of perceptual differences of organizational environments and satisfaction levels among ethnically different employees in today's organizations. These findings are significant as they come in the face of the increasing cultural diversity which pervades almost every facet of the nation. This study has acknowledged that already major corporations have embarked on programs of change as they attempt to realign their corporate cultures to support the cultural diversity which is evidently growing. We see in the predictions of Henry (1990), that by the end of the 20th century, the Hispanic population will have increased by 21%, Asians by 22% , Blacks by 12% and whites by just over 2%.

This chapter discusses the implication of the survey results on the quest for diversity in organizational cultures. The theoretical implication of the results and the study's limitations are discussed. Recommendations are also made for further research in the area.

Cultural diversity can not, by any means, be ignored by politicians, economists, legislators, or educators since cultural diversity will inevitably pervade all institutions in this society. The classroom certainly is one of those places that will feel the impact of this demographic change and will become the institution that is expected to prepare individuals for the impact of that change. Consequently, educational institutions must be prepared for the challenge. What are the cultural dynamics that educational policy makers must confront as they prepare to undertake the task of creating educational cultures that yield positive ethnic relations? What cultural dynamics must they confront to undertake that challenge of adequately preparing graduates to enter the organizational cultures that demand sensitivities and understanding of intercultural/interethnic relationships? The findings of studies such as the current one are starting points of such understandings. The author assumes that these understandings begin with a knowledge of the effect of an individual's ethnicity on his/her perceptions of the organizational climate or his/her psychological climate (PC) perceptions which consequently determine the level of his/her satisfaction with the organization. It is on this assumption that this discussion ensues.

The Extent of PC Perception Differences and Implications for the New Organizational Cultures

The extent of the perceptual differences among the three ethnic groups in this research setting offers some optimism to researchers investigating the influence of ethnicity on perceptual differences in educational environments. African-American, Latin American, and White American students share almost similar perceptions of those aspects of the educational environment that relate to relationships with instructors, instructors' styles, instructors' treatment of all students, relationships with and usefulness of academic counseling and non-academic counseling, among other factors. In accordance with the premise that underlies the theory of PC perception, this consensuality of perceptions implies that members of these groups employ similar cognitive frames and informational processes in perceiving the realities of these environmental dimensions. The broader implication of this consensuality of perception is that students' perception of dimensions of an educational environment have been shaped by a scholastic ethnicity that Longstreet (1978) suggests is shared by all students who have been educated in the same school system. For example, the majority of African-American, Latin American, and White American students have been educated in the US school system and have consequently learned the dynamics of the US educational environment in the same way.

Their cognitive frames have also been shaped by a scholastic ethnicity that allows for a commonality of perceptions in this type of environment.

However, the significant interethnic differences in perception of the quality, nature, and extent of relationships among students in the college is a source of concern. This finding implies that even though students perceive the college environment in similar ways, they experience differences in that aspect of the college climate that deals with students' relationships. In accordance with the theory of PC perception, through a process of cognitive constructions, each student in the research setting will inevitably interpret situations or events in the environment in ways that are psychologically meaningful to him/her. The theory also postulates that PC perceptions are a function of the person by the situation (PXS) interaction. These findings suggest that as the students interact with others in the environment, it is their ethnicity that influences the meaning they give to the nature, extent, and quality of the relationship. This implies that PC perceptions of this aspect of the environment is determined by ethnicity.

The general implication of this finding for new organizational cultural shifts is that the relationship among ethnic groups remains a dynamic that requires vigorous and in-depth investigation and treatment if genuine changes are to be made to support the new and pervasive cultural diversity in institutions. The heart of the organization is its members who must work effectively together to keep the organization productive. If organizational members do not perceive their relationships in similar ways, there will be the potential for mistrust, disrespect, and discord among ethnically different organizational members. These are certainly not attributes that yield a positive climate for the organizational cultural change on which organizations ought to be embarking. The PC perception findings in this research setting indicate a need for intercultural communication assessments among ethnically different organizational members prior to the institution of any cultural diversity programs in the organization. In the case of the higher education institution, the emphasis on stimulating intercultural communications and understanding needs to be centered on aspects of the college life that are meaningful to students of college age, for example, social events, non-academic organizations, fraternities and sororities.

The findings of significant differences in PC perception within the ethnic groups indicate a homogeneity among African-American students and among White American students as reflected in their perceptions of the environment. There are more significant differences in PC perception among Latin American students than the other two groups. This may be so because there are more students in this group than in the other ethnic groups who were born in Latin America and whose parents were born there also. Latin American and the Caribbean is in itself a culturally diverse region, becoming so following the decolonialization era. Indians, Spanish, and African settlers were transformed into the individual who is known today as "Hispanic." As a consequence, the society became a multicultural one characterized by Spanish, Indian, and African retentions. Respondents from this region will tend to be less homogeneous that African-American respondents and White American respondents who interethnically share a monoculture in the US.

It is interesting that African-American and Latin American respondents who were not born in the US share similar perceptions about the extent of equity in treatment of all students by instructors. These perceptions are significantly more negative than those of their colleagues who were born in the US. This, however, is the only dimension in which there was a consensus of perceptions among the subgroups of ethnic groups. African-American respondents differ in three PC scales as a result of three subgroups; Latin Americans differ in 9 PC scales as a result of four subgroups; and White American respondents differ as a result of two subgroups in two PC scales.

The implication of this finding for organizational cultural shifts is that the Latin American or "Hispanic" culture should not be treated as a singular and monolithic culture as it is currently the tendency to do. If attempts at affecting cultural shifts in organizations to yield truly multicultural organizations are genuine, then sensitivities towards the diversity of the Latin American culture are important.

Conclusively, the PC dimensions that determine satisfaction with the college among the three ethnic respondent groups are diverse. Findings imply that the satisfaction of African-American and Latin American students is strongly contingent on only four PC dimensions in the college environment, while White students' satisfaction is moderately contingent on 10 PC dimensions in the environment. This is particularly important to investigations of ethnic differences in organizations, since organizational experts are very aware of the fact that satisfied employees are critical to the ultimate success of the organization. Understanding the predictors of satisfaction with organizations for each ethnic group means having the knowledge of what dimensions of the environment are meaningful to them.

In the current research setting, no one dimension of the environment is a common predictor of the satisfaction of all three ethnic groups. White American and African-American students share two predictors of satisfaction. However, one of the predictors, "general support of all students by instructor" while having a strong positive relation with satisfaction for African-American students has an even stronger but negative relationship with satisfaction for White American respondents. This implies that while African-American students feel more satisfied when they perceive that instructors are supportive of all students, White American students are conversely dissatisfied when they perceive that instructors are supportive of all students.

White American and Latin American students share two predictors of satisfaction with "fairness in treatment of all students by instructors" being negatively related to satisfaction for both groups. This implies that these two ethnic groups are more satisfied with college when they perceive an inequality of treatment of all students by the instructors. African-American and Latin American students share one predictor of satisfaction. They both need to perceive positive relations among students to be satisfied with college. These findings imply that White American and Latin American students in this research setting seem to need preferential treatment by instructors to be satisfied with college. This is noteworthy, since fairness in treatment of culturally diverse organizational members is an important ingredient in any organization whose success is contingent on its members. If some members' satisfaction with the organization is determined by their perceived unfairness of treatment of some organizational members, then the notion of an effective culturally diverse organization is nonexistent.

The implications of the findings of this study in this research setting are that an attempt at organization cultural shifts that accommodate a growing cultural diversity will not be without its problems. Lack of perceptual agreement among the three ethnic groups with respect to the quality, extent, and the nature of relationships among students illuminates the fact that all groups of students do not enjoy the same experiences in their relationships with students on the campus. The PC dimensions of the environment in which significant perceptual differences are found between African-American and White American respondents reflect that these two groups do not perceive interaction facilitation by instructors, cooperation, competition, and relationships among students in the same ways. In fact, Latin American and White American students perceive significant differences in the extent of cooperation among students in the college.

The implication is that African-Americans perceive competition among students which induces mistrust and lack of cooperation and harmony as inevitably affecting relationships among students. They also perceive that instructors do nothing to facilitate interaction among the groups. Latin American students perceive less cooperation, trust, and harmony among students than White American respondents. They too perceive more competition and less positive relationships among students in the college than White students do.

Like most organizations in the United States, this is a predominantly white college with white American students experiencing the most comfort in relationships among students on the campus. Because of their predominance, White American students are not as influenced by the other two ethnic groups as much as these ethnic groups are influenced by them. An inevitable assimilation process takes place as African-Americans and Latin Americans enter a predominately white organization. In this research setting, the campus organizations are essentially white dominated; there is an absence of African-American fraternities or sororities and an absence of African-American students in the existing ones. The Latin American fraternity and sorority, although quite new, are vibrant and are serving to mobilize and consolidate the Latin American students into a group that is becoming an important part of the college environment.

An emphasis on cultural diversity in an organization is expected to yield an environment in which members of different cultures learn about, understand, and consequently respect what each other stands for or identifies with. If an ethnic group has no vibrant organizations, societies, or clubs in a culturally diverse environment, they, consequently, have no identification in that particular environment; there are no means of cohesion that would identify them as an ethnic unit. They will then offer very little to cultural diversity in organizations. This is the situation that African-American students encounter in this research setting. This lack of cohesion as a group influences their feelings of not being a critical part of the organization. This absence of feeling of belongingness will also affect their pride in and satisfaction with the college, as the findings reflect. Latin American students experience the most pride in and satisfaction with college among the three ethnic groups; this may be an attribute of the strength of their ethnic organizations on the campus which stimulate their sense of belonging to the college environment.

Conclusively, the potential for genuine cultural diversity will grow if all ethnic groups within organizations are cohesive and vibrant enough to contribute significant, if not equal, aspects of their ethnicity to the organizational culture. It is not until such time that mutual respect, sensitivities, and understandings of each other will improve. These are some of the ingredients for improved relationships within organizations and among students on college campuses.

Theoretical Implications of the Findings of the Study

The findings of the current study have implications for the conceptual framework from which this study evolved. The study postulated that ethnicity is a significant determinant of psychological climate (PC) perception. It employed Longstreet's (1978) hypothesis of the development of ethnicity and applied it to the premises of PC theory.

The conceptual framework

This study proceeded from a conceptual framework which posited that psychological climate perceptions are a function of the individual's interaction with his/her environment (PXS). The individual has a cognitive structure provided by his/her family, scholastic, and national ethnicity, as Longstreet (1978) believes. This, in turn, shapes his/her perception of the world, according to Samovar and Porter (1991,1991). As James and Jones (1978) postulate as the individual interacts with his/her organizational environment, he/she employs these cognitive constructions giving psychological meaning to situations or events that occur in the environment.

The findings of this survey moderately support the conceptual framework from which this study departs. Differences in PC perception and satisfaction are found among and within the ethnic respondent groups in this research setting. There is significant lack of perceptual agreement in only four PC scales which all define that aspect of the environment that deals with the extent, nature, and quality of the relationships among students. There are similarities in perceptions among the ethnic groups about the other aspects of the college environment.

Taken together, these findings do not provide significant support for the conceptual framework that the study advances. If ethnicity is indeed a determinant of PC perception, the study would have concluded significant PC perceptual differences in more aspects of the college environment. However, the consensus of PC perceptions among the groups in some areas and the significance of PC perceptual differences in that one area seems to suggest that there are other interacting variables that may occur within the relationship between ethnicity and PC perception that have not been taken into account. The strength of ethnicity in predicting PC perception probably diminishes as ethnicity interacts with intervening variables in the environment. This phenomenon deserves further investigation in this research setting.

The findings of significant PC perceptual differences within the ethnic groups lend some support to the study's conceptual framework with regard to the contribution of family, scholastic, and national ethnicity to the development of ethnicity. The subgroups within the ethnic groups in which significant differences are found are the following: location and types of high schools attended, the country of birth, and the country of parents' birth. There are no significant differences in a significant number of PC scales. Consequently, the support for the relationship of the ethnic development hypothesis with relation to PC perception is not very strong.

However, there is another way to view these findings that will give credence to the relationship between the ethnic development hypothesis and PC perception, and that is to compare the extent of differences within ethnic groups and the extent of diversity within the groups. Results show that the most significant PC perception differences occur among the Latin American student group. This is the most diverse group in this research setting, with a little more than half of its students being born in the US while the others are immigrants from varied Latin American countries. The least amount of significant perceptual differences occur within the White student group, which is the most homogeneous, with only two of the respondents in this group being born out of the US.

In accordance with Longstreet's ethnicity hypothesis, students who are born in the same country, attended the same type of high schools, and come from similar historical family backgrounds will share similar ethnicities. This study's conceptual framework then suggests that these students will share similar PC perceptions of the college environment. Although the significant differences within these subgroups were few, it is noteworthy that the highest number of differences occur within the most diverse ethnic student group and the lowest number of differences occur within the least diverse student group in this research setting.

There certainly are differences in satisfaction with college among the ethnic groups, with Latin American students being the most satisfied and African-American students being the least satisfied. The study concludes that the differences in the PC perception scales that predict satisfaction for each group reflect that there are differing aspects of the college environment that are meaningful to each ethnic group. These differences are in part a function of the status that each group holds in a nation that has a history, past and present, characterized by racial segregation and racial prejudices.

The findings of the study clearly show that in general, African-American students' satisfaction with the college is contingent upon the need to perceive the college environment as equally supportive to all students and as one in which there are positive student relations and interethnic group interactions. In other words, they need to experience an equality in all relationships on the campus. In order to be satisfied, Latin American students also need to perceive an environment in which relationships among students are positive. However, they must also be in an environment in which instructors do not necessarily exercise fairness with all students but are supportive of their needs. White American students satisfaction with college is contingent upon 11 PC perception predictors. Interestingly, those predictors do not mirror any of those found for African-American students, with the exception of the negative relationship between counseling and satisfaction. Yet another noteworthy finding is the reversal of the role of "general support" for both these groups. African-American students need to perceive an environment that supports all students in order to be satisfied, while White American students need to perceive an environment that does not equally support all students in order to be satisfied with college. Of the four predictors of Latin American students' satisfaction, two of them are shared by White American students. They are the need to perceive instructors as not fair in treatment of all students and the need to perceive that instructors are supportive of their needs.

These findings suggest that there is a dynamic that underlies the nature of the predictors of satisfaction for each of these groups. Further investigation in this area will serve to highlight the phenomenon.

Limitations of the Study

The generalizability of the present study is called into question as the survey items are constructed for and limited to educational environments; this survey instrument cannot be used in the work environment without modification. The study is also limited in that its findings may still not be generalizable to educational institutions. This study was conducted on a predominantly white campus located in the suburbs of New Jersey. Research that attempts to duplicate the efforts of the present study must take certain characteristics of the environment into consideration. Results of a study similar to the present one may differ as a consequence of the ethnicity of the predominant group on campus and as a result of academic status of the students; in addition, undergraduate students may yield different results than graduate students. Another study of this nature may also yield different results because of the location of the campus. The possibility does exist that ethnic groups of people are different in different parts of the country and even in different areas of a given state.

The sample size for the White respondent subgroups with regard to country of birth and country of parents' birth may also be a source of limitation for the study. This sample size was significantly small and as a result the conclusions with reference to significant PC perceptual differences within these subgroups of this sample cannot be given credence. The sample size for the same subgroups of African-American respondents can potentially be another limitation for the study. This sample size was more significant than that of the white respondents but relatively smaller than that of the Latin American respondents. However, the conclusions from these findings may be drawn with guarded confidence.

Recommendations for Further Research

Further research of this type needs to be conducted not only in other educational institutes but also in work environments. After all, ethnic diversity has begun to pervade the work establishments of the US; consequently, research in ethnicity will become the primary medium through which people will begin to understand and respect each other as they are compelled to work together.

Of interest to any investigator in this field is this study's conclusion that ethnicity does influence the PC perception of certain aspects of the environment and not others. Further studies ought to concentrate on the reasons for these differences. Researchers may begin by determining if there are variables that intervene in the relationship between ethnicity and PC perception, and, if so, the nature of those variables should be investigated.

Surely, another area of interest to researchers in the field is the intra-ethnic diversity of PC perception of the environment. Further investigation employing Longstreet's (1978) ethnicity development hypothesis should focus on determining the extent of perceptual diversity that exists within ethnic groups. Each of the variables in this hypothesis should be tested in an attempt to assess the strength of each in the development of ethnicity; their influence in the relationship between ethnicity and PC perception within ethnic groups should also be assessed.

This study has only touched the surface of a new focus on the influence of ethnicity on the development of PC perceptions in organizations. The influence of ethnicity in psychological climate perceptions in organizations cannot be ignored in the face of a demographically changing nation with regard to ethnic composition. Further research in this organizational phenomenon is a must.

Summary

This study has contributed to the cornerstone of the building of a predicted body of research that will investigate the dynamics of ethnicity in the development of psychological climate perceptions specifically of members of organizations. An extended literature review reflected a deficiency in the large body of research on PC climate. That deficiency pertained to the influence or role of ethnicity/culture in the development of an organizational member's PC perception. Past research reveals the investigation of the influence on PC perceptions of organizational members' "position in the organization," their "levels of remunerations," their "role requirements," their "seniority," and the "behavior of their leaders," among other variables. However, the influence of members' ethnicity has been neglected.

This study investigated ethnicity's impact on psychological climate perceptions among students in a private four year college located in the suburbs of southern New Jersey. Ninety-eight African-American students, 98 White American students and 59 Latin American students completed a 14-page questionnaire that sought to determine if (1) psychological climate (PC) perceptions vary among African-American, Latin American, and White American students; (2) psychological climate (PC) perceptions vary among subgroups within African-American students groups, Latin American student groups, and White American student group with regard to (a) the type of high school they attended, (b) the location of the high school they attended, (c) their country of birth, (d) the country of their parents' birth and (e) their gender; and (3) there is a relationship between students' ethnicity, PC perceptions and concomitant satisfaction with the college.

Chapter 8

Conclusions

Scholars currently devise methods and mechanisms in an attempt to construct institutional climates that favor cultural diversity; they must, however, keep in mind that it is the environmental perceptions or psychological climate perceptions of the organizational members that determine the possibility for genuine positive relations between the culturally diverse in any organization. The results of this study may stimulate mixed feelings for those who are optimistic about the potential for a smooth realignment of organizational cultures that allow for environments in which a culturally diverse work force can truly work harmoniously together.

The study offers optimism in its findings of no significant differences in psychological climate (PC) perceptions among the three ethnic groups with reference to academic and non-academic counseling, instructors' support and treatment of all students and classroom climate. This lends support to the conclusions of Astin (1982) and Cheatham et al. (1984) that there is a convergence of perceptions between black and white students concerning campus ambience, institutional policies, as well as a similarity in academic and career goals. The similarity in perceptions of these aspects of the environment suggests that there is support for the traditional view that climate is a characteristic of the organization. It suggests some objectivity in the existence of a climate in certain aspects of the environment that will inevitably be perceived in the same way by ethnically different organizational members. If this is so, then the organization with a truly culturally diverse work force should only concern itself with establishing a management style conducive to the satisfaction and happiness of its members. However, this study's findings suggest that the dynamics of organizational climate are less objective than some scholars postulate.

Significant differences in psychological perceptions were found among the three ethnic groups with regard to that aspect of the environment that defines the nature, quality, and harmony of the relationship among students on the campus. This finding, on the other hand, supports psychological climate (PC) theory's postulation that different ethnic groups possess different cognitive structures that allow them to perceive the same aspects of the environment in different ways. It is, consequently, that obstacle with which proponents of organizational culture realignment must contend.

The significant perceptual differences in this aspect of the environment suggest that ethnically different students have different experiences in relationships and different ways of defining a positive relationship; consequently, they perceive the relationships among students in the college differently. The finding may also suggest that as Willie and Levy (1972) noted, there is still a separatism between black and white and, in this case, Latin American students in the same environment which may lead to different college-related experiences and, consequently, different PC perceptions. Either conclusion illuminates the fact that ethnically different groups do not define relationships in the same way. The relationship among ethnically diverse organizational members is one of the critical aspects of the foundation on which a successful culturally diverse organization is built. If the relationship among members is important to the satisfaction of any ethnic group that perceives it as negative, the success of the organization is in jeopardy. Scholars in the field must concern themselves with this aspect of the organizational environment and how it is perceived by its ethnically different members.

Determining the aspects of the environment that are meaningful to the different ethnic groups translates into understanding what environmental conditions determine the satisfaction of its members. As revealed in this study's findings, the predictors of satisfaction for each of the three ethnic groups are dissimilar. Of significance to studies in this area is the finding that African-American students perceive all aspects of the relationship among students in the college significantly more negatively that White American students, while their satisfaction with college is determined by their perception of positive relationships among students. The repercussions of this may be damaging to the well-being of the organizational member and may affect his/her performance in the organization.

Although this study is a preliminary one and may be limited in its generalizability, it provides some insight into the possible PC perceptions among ethnically different organizational members. It is imperative that organizational scholars invest significant research efforts in preparing organizations for the rapidly growing visibility of the minority population in the "American tapestry." It is imperative that they consistently test the psychological climate of organizations with special emphasis on those in the educational institutions. Educators must understand that one of their major objectives in the system is to graduate a student body that is adequately prepared to enter the culturally diverse work environment in which sensitivities, respect, and understanding for ethnically different people is aimportant qualification for success.

Climate has traditionally been viewed as a characteristic of the organization; this study has employed it as a characteristic of the individual in an attempt to determine if variances in perception of different ethnic groups of students exist with regards to specific areas of the organizational environment. The findings theoretically suggest that organizational and psychological climate in the same environment are not mutually exclusive. There are aspects of an environment that by nature are easily subjected to nuances in personal perceptions while there are other aspects that characterize the organization that are not.

This author can only hope that the efforts of interculturalist and organizational scholars, combined with the fervency of the few proponents of organizational culture realignment, can stimulate the interest of key educational policy makers in creating educational climates in which future organizational members can be exposed to and appreciate cultural diversity. Intercultural studies incorporated into the curriculum is not enough. There must also be an insurance that ethnic groups on school campuses are socially, educationally, and culturally organized. Organization of ethnic groups on a campus may be viewed by some as a method of isolation and segregation from other cultures on the campus, but organization of individuals serve to promote a feeling of strength and belongingness. That perceived strength as a group can translate into members feeling that they belong to a group that is an integral part of the organization's existence. Students achieving self worth and self esteem would be the result of this effort. It is with that strength and improved self-esteem that an ethnic group on any campus can be motivated to share in the cultures of others and to share its culture with others. For the sake of the "browning of America," separatism for the sake of collectivity is worth at least one try.

Bibliography

Adams, B. (1970). Isolation, function and beyond: American kinship in the 1960's. *Journal of Marriage and the Family,* 32, 575-598.

Adler, N. J. (1986) *International dimension of organizational behavior.* Boston: Kent Publishing, Cl.

Allaire, Y., & Firsirotu, M. E. (1984). Theories of organizational culture. *Organization Studies,* 5, 193-226.

American Council of Education. (1988). *One third of a nation: A report of the commission on minority participation in education and American life.* Washington, DC.

Angle, H. L., & Perry, J. L. (1986). Dual commitment and labor-management relationship climates. *Academy of Management Journal,* 29, 31-50.

Argyris, C. (1957). *Personality and organization.* New York: Harper & Row.

Argyle, M., & Little, B. R., (1972). Do personality traits apply to social behavior? *Journal for the Theory of Social Behavior,* 2.1 1-35.

Astin, A. S. (1968). *The college environment.* Washington, DC: American Council on Education.

Astin, A. S., Holland, J. L. (1961). The environmental assessment technique: A way to measure college environments. *Journal of Educational Psychology,* 52, 308-316.

Astin, A. W. (1982). *Minorities in higher education.* San Fransisco: Jossey-Bass.

Atkins, D., Morten, G., and WingSue, D. (1983). *Counseling american minorities: A cross-cultural perspective.* Dubuque, IA: William C. Brown, Co.

Babbit, C. E., & Burbach, H. J. (1979). Perceptions of social control among black college students. *Journal of Negro Educaton, 48*(1), 37-42.

Bagozzi. R. P., & Phillips, L. W. (1982). Representing and testing organizational theories: A holistic control. *Administrative Science Quarterly 27,* 459-489.

Bandura, A. (1978). The self system in reciprocal determination. *American Psychologist, 33,* 344-358.

Barker , R. G. (1968). *Ecological psychology: Concepts and methods for studying the environment of human behavior.* Stanford, CA: Stanford University Press.

Baron, R. N. (1981). Social knowing from an ecological event perspective: A consideration of the relative domains of power for cognitive and perceptual modes of knowing. In Z. H. Harvey (ed.) *Cognition, Social Behavior and the Environment* (pp 612-89) Hillsdale, NJ: Brlbaum.

Bernard, J. (1966). *Marriage and family among negroes.* Englewood Cliffs, NJ: Prentice Hall.

Berry, J. W. (1976). *Applied cross-cultural psychology.*

Blassingame, J. W. (ed.) (1971). *New perspectives on black studies.* University of Illinois Press.

Blumer, H. (1962). Society as symbolic interaction. In A.M. Rose (Ed.). *Human behavior and social process.* (pp 179-192). Boston: Houghton-Mifflin.

Blumer, H. (1969). *Symbolic interactionism: Perspective and method.* Englewood Cliffs. NJ: Prentice-Hall.

Boldland, W. R. (1971). Size, organization and environmental mediation: A study of colleges and universities. In. W. Heydebrand (ed.) *Comparative Organizations: The Results of Empirical Research.* Englewood Cliffs, NJ:Prentice Hall.

Bonilla, E. S. (1964). *Interaccion social y personalidad en una communidad de Puerto Rico:* San Juan, PR: Ediciones Juan Ponce de Leon.

Bowers, K. S. (1973). Situationism in psychology: An analysis and a critique. *Psychological Review, 80,* 307-336.

Bridgman, P. W. (1959). *The way things are.* Cambridge: Harvard U. Press.

Browser, B. P., & Hunt, R. (1981). *Impacts of racism on white Americans.* London, England; Beverly Hills, CA.

Burback, H. J., & Thompson, M. A. (1971). Alienation among college freshmen: A comparison of puerto rican, black and white students. *Journal of College Student Personnel, 12,* 248-252.

Bushnell, J. H. (1962). Student culture at vassar. In N. Sanford (ed.) *The American College: A Psychological and Social Interpretation of the Higher Learning.* New York:Wiley.

Campbell, J. P., Dunnette, M. D., Lawler, E. E. III, & Weick, K. E. Jr. (1970). M*anagerial behavior performance and effectiveness,* New York:Mc Graw-Hill.

Centra, J. A., & Rock, D. (1971). College environments and student academic achievement. *American Education Research Journal,* 8, 623-634

Chachere, E. C., & Elliot, R. J. (1977). Perceptual dissonance and inner-city education. J*ournal of Negro Education, 46*(3), 329-333.

Cheatham, H. E. (1986). Equal access: Progress or retrogression. *Journal of College Student Personnel,* 27(3), 202-204.

Cheatham, H. E., Levine, V., & Thomas, J. A.W. (1984). *Factors in black student retention: Two campuses compared.* Unpublished report to Equal Opportunity Planning Committee, The Pennysylvania State University, University Park.

Chickering, A. W. (1969). *Education and identity.* San Francisco, CA: Jossey-Bass.

Chivers, T. S. (1988). *Race and culture in education: Issues arising from the swann committee report.* Nfer-Nelson, England.

Cisco-Titi, M. (1990). *Stereotyping, social distance and language attitudes as factors in communication among Africans, African American and African Caribbean university students.* Doctoral Dissertation, Howard University, Washington, DC.

Clark, B. R., & Trow, M. (1966). The organizational context. In T. M. Newcomb and E. K. Wilson (eds.) *College Peer Groups: Problems and Prospects for Research.* (pp. 17-20). Chicago, IL: Aldine.

Coll, C.T.G. (1990). Developmental outcome of minority infants: A process-oriented look into our beginnings. *Child Development,* 61, 270-289.

Cooper, H. M., & Good, T. L. (1983) *Pygmation grows up: Studies in the expectation communication process,* New York, NY, Longman Inc.

Cuyjet, M. J. (1986). True for some black students, but not for all. *Journal of College Student Personnel,* 27(3), 204-205.

Davis, J. A. (163). Intellectual climates in 135 American college and universities: At study in social psychologies. *Sociology of Education,* 37, 110-128.

Diaz-Guerrero, R. (1967). Psychology of the Mexican. In Joan Moore and Harry Pachon. H*ispanics in the United States,* (pp. 125-126). Englewood Cliffs. NJ: Prentice Hall.

Drexler, J. A. Jr. (1977). Organizational climate: Its homogeneity within organizations. J*ournal of Applied Psychology,* 62, 38-42.

Dubois, W. E. B. (1961). *The souls of black folk.* NY: Fawcett Publications.

Duignae, P. J. & Gann, L. H. (1986). *The Hispanics in the United States: A history.* Boulder, CO:Drowell-Collier Publishing Co.

Dye, E. H., & Harris A. C. (1990). Changing just impressions: The effect of a short-term initial encounter in a multi-cultural classroom. T*he Howard Journal of Communications,* 2(3), 276-285.

Dye, E. H., & Harris A. C. (1986). Determination of the reliability of organizational climate. *Psychology and Praxis, 30*(3), 116-124.

Dye, E. H., & Harris A. C. (1984). Quantitative evaluation of the climate of an organization. R*evue de Psych Applique,* 34(2), 149-172.

Dye, E. H., & Harris A. C. (1982). Psychological climate and psychological atmosphere of the collective body. S*hidia-Psycholgica,* 24(3-4), 301.

Ekehammer, B. (1974). Interactionism in personality from a historical perspective. P*sychological Bulletin,* 81, 1026-1048.

Endler, N. S., & Magnusson, D. (1976). Toward an interactional psychology of personality. P*sychological Bulletin,* 83, 956-974.

Erdelyi, M. H. (1974). A new look at the new look: Perceptual defense and vigilance. P*sychological Review, 81,* 1-25.

Feldman, K. A. (1971). Measuring college environments: Some uses of path analysis. A*merican Education Research Journal,* 8,(1) 51-70.

Feldman, K. A. (1969). Studying the impacts of colleges on students. *Sociology of Education,* 42, 207-237.

Femminella, F. X. (1979) *Education and ethnicity. "Euro-ethnics in Anglo-ethnic schools.* Statement made at a consultation sponsored by the US Commission of Civil Rights." Chicago, Illinois.

Fieg, J. P., & Blair, J. G. (1980). T*here is a difference: 17 intercultural perspectives.* Washington, DC:Meridian House International.

Fitzpatrick, J. P. (1976). The Puerto Rican family. In C.H. Mindel and R.W. Habenstein (Eds.). *Ethnic families in America: Patterns and variations.* New York: Elsevier.

Fleming, J. (1984). *Blacks in college.* San Francisco: Josey-Bass.

Forehand, G. A., & Gilmer, B.V.H. (1964). Environmental variation in studies of organizational behavior. *Psychological Bulletin, 62,* 361-382.

Frichette, S. (1976). *Factor associated with the social climate of single-sex and coeducational residence halls, fraternities, and sororities on the Oregon State University campus.* Unpublished Doctoral Dissertation, Oregon State University.

Funkenstein, D. H. (1962). Failure to graduate from medical school. *Journal of Medical Education,* 37. 585-603.

Garcia Call, C. T. (1990). Developmental outcome of minority infants: A process-oriented look Into our beginnings. *Child Development, 61,* 270-289.

Garza, R. T., & Nelson, D. B. (1973) A comparison of mexican and anglo-american perceptions of the university environment. *Journal of College Student Personnel,* 14, 399-401.

Gavin, J. F. & Howe, J. G. (1975). Psychological climate: Some theoretical and empirical considerations. *Behavioral Science,* 20(4) 228-240.

Gavin, J. F., (1975). Organizational climate as a function of personal and organizational variable. *Journal of Applied Psychology,* 60, 135-139.

Gerst, M., & Moos, R. H. (1972) The social ecology of university student residences. *Journal of Educational Psychology* 63, 513-525.

Gibbs, J. T. (1973). Black students/white university: Different expectations. *Personnel and Guidance Journal,* 51, 463-469.

Gillespie, J. M., & Allport, G.W. (1955). *Youth's outlook on the future.* New York: Doubleday.

Glasheen, J. (1989). Who inspires diversity? *Hispanic Business, Oct. 1989.*

Glick, W. H. (1985).Conceptualizing and measuring organizational and psychological climate: Pitfalls in multilevel research. *Academy of Management Review,* 10, 601-616.

Goldsen, R. K., Rosenberg, M., Williams, R. M. Jr., & Schuman, E. A. (1960). *What college students think.* Princeton:Van Nostrand.

Goodwin, G. C. (1982) A long term study of the differential perceptions of a university climate: Student groups. *College Student Journal,* 16(3), 220-225.

Greene, M. (ed.) (1989). *Minorities on campus: A handbook for enhancing diversity.* American Council on Education, Washington, DC.

Greene, M. F. (ed.) (1989). *Minorities on campus.* Washington,

DC:American Council on Education.

Guion, R. M. (1973). A note on organizational climate. *Organizational Behavior and Human Performance*, 9, 120-125.

Hall, E. T. (1977). *Beyond culture*. Garden City, NY:Anchor Press.

Halpin, A. W., & Croft, D. B. (1963) *The organizational cimate of schools*. Chicago:University of Chicago Press.

Harper, F. D. (1969). Black student revolt on the white campus, *Journal of College Student Personnel*, 9, 291-295.

Hater, J. J. (1971). *Agreement among perceptions of psychobiology climate: A comparison of within groups and between group designs*. Unpublished Thesis, Texas Christian University.

Hedegard, J. M., & Brown, D. R. (1969). Encounters of some negro and white freshman with a public multiversity. *Journal of Social Issues*, 25(3), 131-144.

Heist, P. (1960). Diversity in college student characteristics. *Journal of Educational Sociology*, 33, 279-291.

Hellreigel, D., & Slocum, J. W., Jr., (1974). Organization climate: Measures research and contingencies. *Academy of Management Journal*, 17, 255-280.

Henry, W. A.,111 (1990). "Beyond the melting pot." *Time, April 9.*

Hess, B., Markson, E. W., & Stein, P. J.; (1988). Racial and ethnic minorities: An overview. In P. S. Rothenberg. (ed.) *Racism and Sexism: An Integrated Study* (pp. 88-89). New York: St. Martins Press.

Hornick, C. W., James L. R., & Jones A. P. (1977). Empirical item keying versus a rational approach to analyzing a psychological climate questionnaire. *Applied Psychological Measurement*, 14, 489-500.

Howe, J. G. (1977). Group climate: An exploratory analysis of construct validity. *Organizational Behavior and Human Performance*, 19, 106-125.

Huebner, L. A. (1980). *Interaction of student and campus in university delaware (ed.) student services: A handbook for the profession*. (pp. 117-143) San Francisco, CA: Josey-Bass.

Insel, P. M., & Moos, R. H. (1974). Psychological environments; Expanding the scope of human ecology. *American Psychologists*, 29, 179-188.

Ittleson, W. H., Proshansky, H.M., Rivlin, L.G., & Winkek, G. H. (1974). *An introduction to environmental psychology*. New York: Holt, Reinhart & Winston.

Jacobson, E., Kumata, H., & Gullahorn, J. E. (1962). Cross-cultural psychology. In H.C. Triandis & W.W. Lambert (Eds). *Handbook of Cross-Cultural Psychology* (Vol.1, pp 1-14) Boston: Allyn & Bacon.

Jacobson, E., & Schachter (1954). *Cross-national research: A case study.* Journal of Social Issues, 10. No. 4

James, L. R. (1982). Aggregation bias in estimates of perceptual agreement. J*ournal of Applied Psychology, 67,* 219-229.

James, L. R., Gent, M. J., Hater, J. J., & Coray, K. E. (1979). Correlates of psychological influence: An illustration of the psychological climate approach to work environment perception. P*sychology, 32,* 563-588.

James, L. R., Hartman, E. A., Stebbins, M. W., & Jones, A. P. (1977). An examination of the relationships between psychological climate and VIE model for work motivation. P*ersonnel Psychology,* 30, 229-254.

James, L. R., Hater, J. J., Shanahan, F. M., Bruni, J. R., Irons, D. M., & Sells, S. B. (1980). Identification of perceived environmental factors associated with student adjustment, laboratory performance and satisfaction in the air traffic control specialist training program. Inst*itute of Behavioral Research.* Texas Christian University, Texas:Fort Worth.

James, L. R., Hater, J. J., Gent, M. J., & Bruni, J. R.(1978). Psychological climate: Implications from cognitive social learning theory and interactional psychology. P*ersonnel Psychology*, 312, 783-813.

James, L. R., & Jones, A. P. (1974). Organizational climate: A review of theory and research. P*sychological Bulletin*, 18, 1096-1112.

James, L, R., & Jones, A. P. (1976). Organization structure: A review of structural dimensions and their conceptual relationships with individual attitudes and behavior. O*rganizational Behavior and Human Performance,* 16, 74-113.

James, L.R., Joyce, W. F., & Slocum, J. W. (1988) Comment: Organization do not cognize. A*cademy of Managment Review* 13, 129-132.

James, J. R., & Sells, S. B. (1982) Psychological climate: Theoretical perspectives and empirical research. In D. Magnusson (ed.) T*oward a Psychology of Situations: An International Perspective* (pp. 275-295). Hillsdale, NJ:Erlbaum.

James, J. R., & Sells, S. B. (1981). Psychological climate: Theoretical perspectives and empirical research. In D. Magnusson (ed.) *Toward a Psychology of Situations An Interactional Perspective; Lawrence Erlbaum Associates, NJ: Hillsdale.*

Janosik, S., Creamer, D. G., & Cross, L. H. (1988). The relationship of residence halls' student environment fit and sense of competence. *Journal of College Student Development*, 29(4), 320-326.

Janosik, S. M. (1987). *Relationship of residence hall environments and student sense of competence and academic achievements.* Unpublished doctoral dissertation. Virginia Polytechnic Institution and State University.

Jessor, R. (1981). The perceived environment in psychological theory and research. In D., Magnusson (ed.) T*oward a Psychology of Situation: In Interactional Perspective.* Lawrence Erlhaum Association, NJ:Hillsdale.

Jessor, R., & Jessor, S. L. (1973). The perceived environment in behavioral science. *American Behavioral Scientist*, 16, 801-828.

Jones, A. P., & James, L. R. (1979). Psychological climate: Dimensions and relationships of individual and aggregated work environment perceptions. *Organization Behavior and Human Performance* 23, 201-250.

Jones, A. P., James, L.R., & Bruni, J.R. (1975). Perceived leadership behavior and employee confidence in the leader as moderated by job involvement. J*ournal of Applied Psychology,* 60, 146-149.

Jones, A. P., James, L. R., Bruni, J. R. & Sells, S. B. (1977). Black-white differences in work environment perceptions and job satisfaction and its correlates. P*ersonnel Psychology*, 30, 5-16.

Jones, A. P., Rozelle, R. M. & Svyantek, D. J. (1985) *Organizational climate: An environmental affordances approach.* Unpublished Manuscript: University of Houston.

Jones, E. E., & Gerard, H. B. (1967). *Foundations of social psychology.* New York: Wiley.

Joyce, W. F., & Slocum, J. W. (1984). Collective climates: Agreement as a basis for defining aggregate climates in organizations. *Academy of Management Journal* 27, 721-742.

Joyce, W. F., & Slocum, J. W. (1979). Climates in organizations. In Skerr (ed.) *Organizational Behavior* (pp. 317-336). Columbus, OH:Grid.

Katz, D., & Kahn, R. L. (1966). *The Social Psychology of Organizations.* New York: Wiley.

Katz, J. H. (1989). The challenge of diversity. In C. Woolbright (Ed.). *Valuing diversity on campus: A multicultural approach.* 1-19. Bloomington: Association of College Union-International

Kegan, D. L. (1978). The quality of student life and financial costs: The cost of social isolation. *Journal of College Student Personnel,* 19, 55-58.

Kendall, F. E. (1983). *Diversity in the classroom.* New York:Teachers College Press.

Kerlinger, F. N. (1986). *Foundations of behavioral research.* (3rd. ed.) NewYork:NY CBS College Publishing.

Kim, Y. Y. (1986). *Interethnic communication: Current research.* Newberry Park, CA:Sage Publications.

Kitano, H. H. (1974). *Race relations.* Englewood Cliffs, NJ: Prentice-Hall.

Klemek, J. R., & Hodinko, B. A. (1977). "Psycholized climate of the multicampus community college: A campus amalgam?" *Journal of College Student Personnel,* Nov., 482-485.

Ladner, J. (1971). *Tomorrow's tomorrow.* New York: Anchor Books.

Leicester, M. (1989). *Multicultural education: From theory to practice.* Billing and Sons Ltd. Worcester, Great Britain.

Levine, L. W. (1977). *Black culture and black consciousness: Afro-American thought from slavery to freedom.* Oxford U. Press.

Litwin, G. H. & Stringer, R. A. Jr. (1968). *Motivation and organizational climate.* Boston: Division of Research, Harvard Business School.

Lomotey, Kofi (1990). *Going to school: The Afro-American experience.* State University of New York Press:Albany, NY.

Longstreet, W. (1978). *Aspects of ethnicity: Understanding differences in pluralistic classrooms.* New York, NY:Teachers College Press.

Lynch, J. (1988). *Multicultural education: A global perspective.* Bristol, PA: Taylor & Francis.

Mahoney, M. J. (1977). Reflections on the cognitive learning trend in psychotherapy. *American Psychologist,* 37, 5-13

Marshall, P. (1985). Interpersonal perception variable and communication satisfaction in the classroom. *Communication Research Reports,* 2(1), 90-96.

Matthews, B. (1972). *Black perspectives, Black family and Black community.* A paper delivered to the annual Philosophy Conference, Baltimore, Md.

McCarthy, P. R., & Maier, S. (1983). Effects of race and psychological variables on college student writing. *Journal of Instructional Psychology,* 10(3), 148-157.

McFee, A. (1961). The Relation of students' needs to their perception of the college environment. *Journal Education Psychology,* 52, 25-29

Mischel, W. (1973). Toward a cognitive social learning reconceptualization of personality. *Psychological Review,* 80, 252-283.

Mindel, C. H., & Habenstein, R. W. (eds.). (1976). *Ethnic families in America: Patterns and variations.* New York:NY.

Moore, J., & Pachon, H. (1985). *Hispanics in the united states.* Englewood Cliff, NJ:Prentice-Hall.

Moos, R. H. (1987). Person-environment congruence in work school and health care settings. *Journal of Vocational Behavior,* 31, 231-247.

Moos, R. N. (1986). *Work environment scale manual: Second edition,* Palo Alto, CA: Consulting Psychologists Press.

Moos, R. (1979). *Evaluating educational environments: Procedures, methods, findings and policy implications.* San Francisco, CA: Jossey-Bass.

Moos, R. N. (1976). *The human context: Environmental determinants of behavior.* NY, NY:Wiley.

Moos, R. N., & Geist, M. S. (1974). *University residence environment scale manual.* Palo Alto, CA: Consulting Psychology Press.

Moos, R. N., & Triockett, E. (1987). *Classroom environment scale manual: Second edition.* Palo Alto, CA: Consulting Psychologists Press.

Moussavi, F., Jones, T. W., & Cronan, T. P. (1990). Explaining psychological climate: Is perceptual agreement necessary? *Journal of Social Psychology,* 130(2), 2390-248.

Newman, J. E. (1977). Development of a measure of perceived work environment (PWE). *Academy of Management Journal,* 4, 520-534.

Noel, M. M. & Burbach, H. J. (1978) Black versus white college: A study of the perceptual distinctions of black students. *College Student Journal,* 12(2), 158-163.

Nobles, W. W. (1973). Psychology research and the black self concept: A critical review. *Journal of Social Issues,* 29, 11-31.

Ogbu, J. U. (1981). *Schooling in the ghetto: A cultural-ecological perspective on community and home influences.* Paper presented at NIE Conference on Follow Through, Philadelphia, PA.

Ogbu, J. U. (1985). A cultural ecology of competence among inner-city black. In M. B. Spencer, G. K. Brookins and W. R. Aklen (eds.) *Beginnings: The Sound and Affective Development of Black Children* (pp 45-66) Hillsdale, NJ:Erlbaum.

Ogbu, J. U. (1978). *Minority educational and caste: The American system in cross-cultural perspective.* New York:Harcourt Brace Iavonovich

One-Third of a Nation. *A Report of the Commission on Minority Participation in Education and American Life,* May 1988, American Council on Education.

Ornstein, S. (1986). Organizational symbols: A study of their meanings and influences on perceived psychological climate. *Organizational Behavior and Human Decision Processes, 38,* 207-229.

Pace, C. R., & Hagstrom, W. D. (1969). *The empirical scales: Technical manual* (2nd ed.). Princeton, NJ: Educational Testing Service.

Pace, C. R. (1963). *CUES college and university environment scales.* Princeton, NJ:Educational Testing Service.

Pace, C. R. (1963). *Technical manual (1963): College and university environment scales.* Princeton, NJ:Educational Testing Service.

Pace, C. R., & Stern, G. G. (1958). An approach to the measurement of psychological characteristics of college environments. *Journal Education Psychology, 49,* 269-277.

Patterson, A. M., Sadlaceck, W. E., & Perry, E.W. (1984). Perceptions of Blacks and Hispanics in two campus environments. *Journal of College Student Personnel, 25,* 513-518.

Patterson, C. J., Kupersmidt, J. B., & Vaden, N. A. (1990) "Income level, gender, ethnicity and household composition as predictors of children's school based competence". Chil*d Development,* 61, 485-494.

Patton, J. A. (1955). *A study of the effects of students' acceptance of responsibility and motivation on course behavior.* Dissertation.

Payne, R. L., Fineman, S., & Wall, T. D. (1976). Organizational climate and job satisfaction: A conceptual synthesis. *Organizational Behavior and Human Performance,* 16, 45-62.

Payne, R. L., & Mansfield, R. (1973). Relationships of perceptions of organizational climate to organizational structure, context and hierarchical position. Ad*ministrative Science Quarterly,* 18, 5615-526.

Perlman, I. (1988) *Ethnic differences: Schooling and social structure among Irish, Italians,Jjews and Blacks in an American city 1880-1935.* Melbourne Australia:Cambridge University Press.

Pervin, L. A. (1967). A twenty-college study of student and college interaction using TAPE (Transactional Analysis of Personality and Environment): Rational, reliability and validity. *Journal of ducational Psychology,* 58, 290-302.

Peterson, R. E. (1965). *Technical manual, college student questionnaires.* Princeton, NJ:Educational Testing Service.

Pfeifer, C. M. Jr. (1976). Relationship between scholastic aptitude, perception of university climate, and college success for black and white students. J*ournal of Applied Psychology,* 61, 341-347.

Pfiefer, C. M. Jr., & Schneider, B. (1974). University climate perceptions by black and white students. J*ournal of Applied Psychology,* 59,(3), 660-662.

Poole, M. S., & McPhee, R. D. (1983) A structural analysis of or ganizational climate. In L. L. Putnam and M. E. Pacanowsky (eds.) C*ommunication and Organization: An Interpretive Approach* (pp. 195-219) Beverly Hills, CA:Sage.

Powel, G. N., & Butterfield, D. A. (1978). The case of subsystem climate in organizations. A*cademy of Management Review,* 3, 151-157.

Pruitt, A. S. (1970). Black poor at white colleges: Personal growth goals. *Journal of College Personnel,* 11, 3-7.

Rosen, P. (1980). *The neglected dimension: Ethnicity in American life.* Washington:DC.

Rock, D. A., Centra, J. A., & Linn, R. L. (1970). Relationships between college characteristics and student achievement. A*merican Educational Research Journal,* 1, 109-121.

Rokeach, M. (1973). *The nature of human values.* New York: Free Press.

Rousseau, D. M. (1988). The construction of climate in organizational research. In C. L. Cooper and I. T. Robertson (Eds.) *International Review of Industrial and Organizational Psychology.*

Samovar, L. A., & Porter, R. E. (1991). *Communication between cultures.* CA:Belmont, Wadsworth Inc.

Samovar, L. A., & Porter, R. E. (1991). Basic principles of intercultural communication. In L.A. Samover & R.E. Porter (Eds.) I*ntercultural communication* (6th ed.) (pp. 5-22). CA:Belmont Wadsworth Inc.

Sanford, N. (1966). *The American college*: New York NY: Wiley.

Schein, E. H. (1990). Organizational culture. *American Psychologist, 45,* 109-119.

Schneider, B. (1975). Organizational climate: An essay. *Personnel Psychology,* 28, 447-479.

Schnieder, B., & Bartlet, C. J. (?). Individual differences and organizational climate: The research plan and questionnaire development. P*ersonnel Psychology, 21,* 323-333.

Schnieder, B., Hastof, A. H. & Ellsworth, P. C. (1979). *Person perception* (2nd. ed.) Reading, MA:Addison Wesley.

Schneider, B., Parkington, J. J. & Buston, V. M. (1980). Employee and customer perceptions of service in banks. *Administrative Science Quarterly* 25, 252-267.

Schneider, B., & Reichers, A. E. (1983) On the ecology of climates. *Personnel Psychology,* 36, 19-39.

Sergent, M. T., & Sedlacek,. W. E. (1989) Perceptual mapping: A methodology in the assessment of environmental perceptions. *Journal of College Student Development, 30*(4), 319-322.

Shannon, L., & Shannon, M. (1973). *Minority migrants in the urban community: Mexican-American and negro adjustment to industrial society.* Beverly-Hills, CA: Sage.

Simons, G. (1989). *Working together: How to become more effective in a multicultural organization.* Los Altos, CA:Crisp Publications.

Smircich, L., & Calas, M. B. (1989). Organizational culture: A critical assessment . In F. M. Jablin et al. (Eds.). H*andbook of organizational communication.* (pp 228-263). Sage: CA.

Spencer, M. B. (1990). Development of minority children: An introduction. *Child Development, 61,* 267-269.

Spencer, M. B., & Markstrom-Adams, C. M. (1990) Identity processes among racial and ethnic minority children in America. *Child Development,* 61.

SPSS-X User's Guide (1988), (3rd ed.) SPSS Inc. Chicago, Ill

Staples, R. (1976). The Black American family. In C.H. Mindell and R.W. Habenstein (Eds.). E*thnic families in America.* New York: Elsevier.

Stern, G. G. (1962). The measurement of psychological characteristics of students and learning environments. In S. Messich and J. Ross (eds). M*easurement in Personality and Cognition*, New York:Wiley.

Stevenson, W. H., Chen, C., & Uttal, D. H. (1990). Beliefs and a chievement: A study of black, white and hispanic Children.*Child Development, 61,* 508-523.

Stotland, E., & Canon, L. K. (1972). *Social psychology: A cognitive approach.* Philadelphia, Sanders

Suen, H. K. (1983). Alienation and attrition of black college students on a predominantly white campus. J*ournal of College Student Personnel,* 19, 117-121.

Taylor, C. A. (1986). True for some black students, but not for all. *Journal of College Student Personnel, 27*(3). 204-205.

Taylor, C. A. (1986). Black students on predominantly white college campuses in the 1980s. *Journal of College Student Personnel,* 196-205.

Thomas, R. R. (1992). From affirmative action to affirming diversity. In D. O'Hair and W. F. Gustav (auth.). *Strategic communication in business and professions.* Boston, MA: Houghton Mifflin Co.

Tracey, T. J., & Sherry, P. (1984) College student distress as a function of person environment set. J*ournal of College Student Personnel,* 29(3), 436-442.

Triandis, H. C. (1980a). Introduction to the handbook of cross-cultural psychology. In H.C. Triandis & W.W. Lambert (Eds.), H*andbook of cross-cultural psychology.* (Vol.1, pp1-14) Boston: Allyn & Bacon.

Triandis, H. C., & Albert, R. D. (1989). Cross-cultural perspectives. In F. M. Jablin et. al (Eds.) *Handbook of organizational communication* (pp 264-295) Sage:CA.

US Bureau of the Census (1982) *Census population. 1972-1982.* Washington DC Government, Printng Office.

Verderber, R. F. (1987). *Communicate!* Belmont , CA: Wadsworth.

Walizer, M. H., & Wiener, P. L. (1978). *Research methods and analysis: Searching for relationships.* New York:NY.

Walsh, W. B. (1987). Person environment congruence: A response to the Moos perspective. J*ournal of Vocational Behavior,* 31, 347-352.

Weidman, J. C., & Krus, D. J. (1979). Undergraduate expectations and images of college. P*sychology Reports,* 45, 131-138.

Wells, L. (1982). Effects of ethnicity on the quality of student life: An embedded intergroup analysis. *Yale University; Department of Administrative Science.*

Wells, Leroy, Jr., & Hayles, R. (1980). *Intro-ethnic perceptions among blacks throughout the african diaspora: Some heuristics.* Paper presented at the 13th Annual Convention of the Association of Black Psychologists.

Willie, C. V., & Levy, J. D. (1972). On white campuses black students retreat into separatism. P*sychology Today.*

Willie, C. V., & Levy, J. D. (1972). On white campuses, black students retreat into separatism. A black coed says "white boys are afraid of us." P*sychology Today, March,* 50-80.

Willie, C., & McCord, H. (1973). *Black students at white colleges.* New York:Praegor.

Wilson, W. J. (1980). T*he declining significance of race: Blacks and changing American institutions.* Chicago: University of Chicago Press.

Wimmer, R. D., & Dominick J. R. (1987). M*ass media research: An introduction* (2nd. ed.) CA:Belmont, Wadsworth Publishing Co.

Wolf, P. (1973). International organization and attitude change: A reexamination of the functionalist approach. *International Organization University of Wisconsin Press,* 27, 347-371.

Wright, D. J. (1987) *Responding to the needs of today's minority students.* San Francisco, CA: Josey-Bass, Inc.

Wright, D. (1986). Misrepresenting the black student experience again: A rejoining. *Journal of College Student Personnel,* 27,(3), 206.

Wright, S., & Cowen, E. (1982). Student perception of school environment and its relationship to mood, achievement, popularity and adjustment. A*merican Journal of Community Psychology,* 10, 687-703.

Zohar, D. (1980). Safety climate in industrial organizations: Theoretical and applied implications. J*ournal of Applied Psychology,* 65, 96-102.

Index

About the Author

Wendy V. Lewis Chung is an assistant professor of communication at Rider University in Lawrencville, New Jersey. She received her Ph.D. in Organization Communication from Howard University Her research interests are currently focused on issues relating to the auditing of organizations for diversity, intercultural communication in organizations and organizational diversity.